Seek His Face: Another Year of Old Catholic Homilies

By Robert Mitchell

AF350444

SEEK HIS FACE: ANOTHER YEAR OF OLD CATHOLIC HOMILIES

Written by Robert Mitchell.

First edition. February 2024

Copyright © 2024 Robert Mitchell, all rights reserved.

<u>Also By Robert Mitchell</u>

Lift Up Your Heads: A Year of Old Catholic Homilies

The Wildwood Workbook: Nature Appreciation and Survival

Dedication

To Reverend Harry Bowman, a good seed
standing firm in witness to the truth of the Resurrection

Introduction

The homilies in this volume were all delivered during Ekklesia Epignostika Church and Seminary's online Mass and/or during Holy Communion services broadcast via YouTube live from St. Barachiel Old Catholic Chapel in Richmond, VA (https://www.youtube.com/12thkey/live). Heritage Arts, Inc. is a 501(c)(3), federally-recognized educational charity providing free classes, both in person and online, relating to martial arts, fitness, outdoor skills, and spiritual development.

I am a priest in the Old Catholic tradition. Old Catholics are a relatively small denomination with which many are unfamiliar. In the broadest possible strokes, Old Catholics are a loosely-associated group of sister churches, some in communion with one another and others not, who split from the Roman Catholic Church in the mid-to-late 19th century over various doctrinal and administrative disputes, primarily papal infallibility and the valid appointment of bishops.

There are a number of Old Catholic groups and associations, including the original Old Catholic Church of Utrecht, the German, Austrian, Polish and Swiss Old-Catholic churches, the Polish National Church of America and Canada, the Philippine Independent Church, and so forth. The Declaration of Utrecht (1889) is the doctrinal spine shared by all Old Catholic churches. The opening statement of that document reads,

We adhere faithfully to the Rule of Faith laid down by St. Vincent of Lerins in these terms: "All possible care must be

taken, that we hold that faith which has been believed everywhere, always, by all; for this is truly what is catholic." For this reason we preserve in professing the faith of the primitive Church, as formulated in the oecumenical symbols and specified precisely by the unanimously accepted decisions of the Oecumenical Councils held in the undivided Church of the first thousand years.

Therefore, like the Eastern and Russian Orthodox churches, Old-Catholics recognize the first seven ecumenical councils and the doctrines accepted by the church before the Catholic-Orthodox schism in 1054. Also like the Orthodox churches, Old Catholic priests are allowed to be married. On the other hand, like the Roman Catholic Church, Old Catholics recognize seven sacraments, stress the importance of apostolic succession, and believe in the real presence of Christ in the eucharist. For these reasons and many more, many Old Catholics describe themselves as, "Orthodox but not Eastern, Catholic but not Roman."

Some Old Catholic churches are traditional in terms of doctrine, while others affirm same sex marriage and admit women into the clergy. The Old Catholic churches in the Union of Utrecht, for example, allow female priests and same sex marriage. The Old Catholic Church in the United Kingdom however, which had strong ties to the Church of England in its early days, and is in full communion with the Anglican Communion since 1931, is completely traditional. In the United States, many Old Catholic communions borrow liturgical elements from Anglican Books of Prayer – but this doesn't mean that they align with the Church of England as regards the above issues. Old Catholics in the U.S. range from ultraconservative to ultraliberal.

My Old Catholic seminary is comfortable with a range of viewpoints. Its teachers and bishops tend toward the liberal, while I am drawn to the traditional. I believe it says a great deal about Old

Catholics that we're perfectly comfortable sitting down in pews with people with whom we disagree on some of the finer points. Perhaps this is why the Old Catholic Church often calls itself, "The perfect church for imperfect people." This slogan is one of the many things that drew me to this denomination. I am, you see, very far from perfect.

At age 25, my life was a shambles and my marriage was on the rocks. I blamed it all on my temper. One day I had a fit of road rage so severe that, when I came to myself, it scared me: a simple traffic jam had turned me into a screaming, horn-honking, dash-pounding lunatic. I knew something had to be done. I heard that martial arts lessons would help you get healthy, build discipline, and improve temper. So, I signed up.

Martial arts helped me deal with my personal, emotional, and behavioral issues. I lost weight and gained discipline. But I was still unfulfilled spiritually. So I spent the next 25 years or so exploring various religions (and various martial arts too).

Although I had been raised in a Christian home, and we had been church going when I was very small, that had ended by the time I started elementary school. We always said grace before meals, we read the Bible together and discussed theology, but there was no fellowship or community. So it just made sense to start my quest with Christianity. So I read the Bible cover-to-cover and searched for meaning. But nothing clicked.

I spent almost a year in the Latter-Day Saints, pulling out just one week before I was scheduled to be baptized. I put in several years studying Zen, sitting in meditation for an hour each day. I studied Core Shamanism and went on drumming retreats and on vision quests. I looked into the Unitarian Church. For over five years I practiced solitary Wicca. For two years I was a dedicated student of Qabbalah. I read dozens of books on the subject and completed a five-month multi-disciplinary project involving meditation, art, and weekly fasting.

Decades passed. Eventually certain patterns and common threads shared by many faiths began to emerge. I decided to go back to school and earn a certificate as an interfaith minister or chaplain. As part of the curriculum at Esoteric Interfaith Church, I had to read two books by Alan Watts – <u>Behold the Spirit</u> and <u>Myth and Ritual in Christianity</u> (both written prior to his movement out of the Episcopal priesthood into Eastern Religion). Suddenly everything began falling into place. Thanks to more good books, my patient and loving wife, wise friends, the seminary and its teachers, and by the grace of Father, Son and Holy Ghost, Christianity soon made sense to me in a way that it had never made sense before. My religious quest was over. I immediately entered Ekklesia Epignostika Church & Seminary and began pursuing Holy Orders of the priesthood.

I've told you my story because it informs the perspective of the homilies that follow. If you know that I have had firsthand experience with the negative consequences of disordered thoughts, desires, actions, and beliefs, perhaps it will make me a stronger witness of the Gospel in your eyes. Also, knowing my past should help you understand why I'm more traditional in my views.

I understand how dark and scary it gets, and how fast and severe the fall, when you dance on the edge.

Solemnity of the Most Holy Trinity, June 12, 2022

Readings: Prv 8:22-31, Ps 8:4-5, 6-7, 8-9, Rom 5:1-5, Jn 16:12-15

<u>John 16:12-15 American Standard Version</u>

12 I have yet many things to say unto you, but ye cannot bear them now. 13 Howbeit when he, the Spirit of truth, is come, he shall guide you into all the truth: for he shall not speak from himself; but what things soever he shall hear, these shall he speak: and he shall declare unto you the things that are to come. 14 He shall glorify me: for he shall take of mine, and shall declare it unto you. 15 All things whatsoever the Father hath are mine: therefore said I, that he taketh of mine, and shall declare it unto you.

Today, brothers and sisters, in keeping with an old tradition, we read as our homily the Athanasian Creed. Although scholars are relatively certain that St. Athanasius is not the true author (the most likely candidate is St. Vincent Lérins or another Gaulish priest of the 5th century) the Athanasian Creed has been central to Christianity in the West for 1,500 years.

Throughout the Middle Ages its use in the Roman Catholic Church was frequent and prominent – it was read every Sunday after the Homily. Many Protestant denominations continued that tradition. In the last hundred years or so it has fallen out of favor, probably due to its mention of eternal damnation. But it remains approved for use in both the Roman Catholic Church and Anglican Church, where it is still included in the Book of Common Prayer.

The original was composed in Latin. The English version that given below is from <u>A Manual of Prayers for the Use of the Catholic Laity</u> (1889) by Clarence E. Woodman. To prevent confusion, the original rendering "uncreates" has been modernized by the author to read "uncreated" in keeping with modern usage. All other archaisms have been left intact.

"WHOSOEVER desires to be saved, before all things it is necessary that he hold the Catholic faith. Which faith, except every one do keep entire and inviolate, without doubt he shall perish everlastingly. Now the Catholic Faith is this: that we worship one God in Trinity, and Trinity in Unity. Neither confounding the Persons nor dividing the substance. For there is one Person of the Father, another of the Son, another of the Holy Ghost. But the Godhead of the Father, and of the Son, and of the Holy Ghost is one; the glory equal, the majesty co-eternal. As the Father is, such is the Son, such the Holy Ghost. The Father uncreated, the Son uncreated, the Holy Ghost uncreated. The Father infinite, the Son infinite, the Holy Ghost infinite. The Father eternal, the Son eternal, the Holy Ghost eternal. And yet they are not three eternals, but one Eternal. As also they are not three uncreated, nor three infinites; but one Uncreated, and one Infinite.

In like manner the Father is Almighty, the Son Almighty, and the Holy Ghost Almighty. And yet they are not three almighties, but one Almighty. So the Father is God, the Son God, and the Holy Ghost God. And yet they are not three Gods, but one God. So the Father is Lord, the Son is Lord, and the Holy Ghost is Lord. And yet they are not three Lords, but one Lord.

For as we are obliged by the Christian Truth to acknowledge every Person to be God and Lord: so we are forbidden by the Catholic religion to say there are three Gods or three Lords. The Father was made by no one, neither created, nor begotten. The Son is by the Father alone; not made, nor created, but begotten. The Holy Ghost is from the Father and the Son, not made, nor created, nor begotten, but proceeding. So there is one Father, not three Fathers: one Son, not three Sons: one Holy Ghost, not three Holy Ghosts. And in this Trinity there is nothing before or after, nothing greater or less; but the whole three Persons are co-eternal together and co-equal.

So that in all things, as is aforesaid, the Unity is to be worshipped in Trinity, and the Trinity in Unity. He, therefore, that desires to be saved must thus believe of the Trinity.

Furthermore, it is necessary to everlasting salvation that he also believe faithfully the Incarnation of our Lord Jesus Christ. Now the right faith is, that we believe and confess that our Lord Jesus Christ, the Son of God, is both God and man. He is God of the substance of His Father, begotten before the world; and He is man of the substance of His Mother, born in the world: Perfect God and perfect man; of rational soul and human flesh subsisting, Equal to the Father according to His Divinity; and less than the Father according to His humanity. Who, although He be both God and man, yet He is not two, but one Christ: One, not by conversion of the Godhead into flesh, but by the assuming of human nature unto God: One altogether, not by confusion of substance, but by unity of person.

For as the rational soul and the body constitutes one man, so God and man is one Christ: Who suffered for our salvation, descended into hell, arose again the third day from the dead: He ascended into heaven; He sitteth at the right hand of God the Father Almighty; thence He shall come to judge the living and the dead: At whose coming all men must arise again with their bodies, and must give an account of their own works. And they that have done good shall go into life everlasting;

and they that have done evil into everlasting fire. This is the Catholic faith, which except a man believe faithfully and steadfastly he cannot be saved.

Glory be to the Father, the Son, and the Holy Ghost; as it was in the beginning, is now, and shall ever be, world without end, Amen."

Memorial of the Immaculate Heart of the Blessed Virgin Mary, June 25, 2022

Readings: Lam 2:2, 10-14, 18-19, Ps 74:1b-2, 3-5, 6-7, 20-21, Lk 2:41-51

Luke 2:41-51 American Standard Version

41 And his parents went every year to Jerusalem at the feast of the passover. 42 And when he was twelve years old, they went up after the custom of the feast; 43 and when they had fulfilled the days, as they were returning, the boy Jesus tarried behind in Jerusalem; and his parents knew it not; 44 but supposing him to be in the company, they went a day's journey; and they sought for him among their kinsfolk and acquaintance: 45 and when they found him not, they returned to Jerusalem, seeking for him. 46 And it came to pass, after three days they found him in the temple, sitting in the midst of the teachers, both hearing them, and asking them questions: 47 and all that heard him were amazed at his understanding and his answers. 48 And when they saw him, they were astonished; and his mother said unto him, Son, why hast thou thus dealt with us? behold, thy father and I sought thee sorrowing. 49 And he said unto them, How is it that ye sought me? knew ye not that I must be in my Father's house? 50 And they understood not the saying which he spake unto them. 51 And he went down with them, and came to Nazareth; and he was subject unto them: and his mother kept all these sayings in her heart.

Brothers and sisters, all of us mortals come and go. Having had our day in the sun, night falls upon us and we go to our rest. The secrets in our hearts – our fleeting hopes and fears, our private sins and penances, all of our unspoken thoughts good and bad – die with us. No one will ever know our most private burdens and joys. Who can know what has been in the heart of any mortal once they have passed?

But during the Memorial of the Immaculate Heart of the Blessed Virgin Mary, we meditate upon the mysteries within the heart of the mother of God. What must it have been like for Mary? What were her innermost thoughts, considerations, joys and sorrows? Surely her heart ached under the push and pull of emotional extremes. We can only imagine the awe and fear of being visited by an angel, or the simultaneous joy and burden of being the choice vessel of our Savior Jesus Christ.

We can only wonder what it might have been like watching her son transition into adulthood. Having raised her son from infancy – that is, having instructed and corrected him, having taught him all of the things mothers teach their sons, like how to be patient, to wait his turn, to be polite and use his manners, not to whine and complain, to share his toys with the other children and so on – what must it have been like for her to watch her son slowly transform into the greatest teacher the world had ever known or ever would know? Which of us has the character of the mother of God, who had the humility to accept the teaching of the son she once taught?

Imagine how her heart swelled with faith, joy, and pride as her son performed incredible miracles; then imagine her crushing sadness when witnessing his abandonment, persecution, and torture on a cross. Her heart experienced the crushing agony of receiving the broken, lifeless body of her son as it was lowered from the cross; then, just few days later, her heart must have been swollen to bursting with the unimaginable bliss of seeing him rise from the dead.

No mortal heart has ever suffered the emotional extremes endured by the mother of God. Let us take the day, my friends, to pause and reflect. Let us step into the heart of our mother Mary and walk with her in her great joys and in her great sorrows.

14th Sunday of Ordinary Time, July 3, 2022

Readings: Is 66:10-14c, Ps 66:1-3, 4-5, 6-7, 16, 20, Gal 6:14-18, Lk 10:1-12, 17-20

Luke 10:1-12 American Standard Version

10 Now after these things the Lord appointed seventy [a]others, and sent them two and two before his face into every city and place, whither he himself was about to come. 2 And he said unto them, The harvest indeed is plenteous, but the laborers are few: pray ye therefore the Lord of the harvest, that he send forth laborers into his harvest. 3 Go your ways; behold, I send you forth as lambs in the midst of wolves. 4 Carry no purse, no wallet, no shoes; and salute no man on the way. 5 And into whatsoever house ye shall [b]enter, first say, Peace be to this house. 6 And if a son of peace be there, your peace shall rest upon [c]him: but if not, it shall turn to you again. 7 And in that same house remain, eating and drinking such things as they give: for the laborer is worthy of his hire. Go not from house to house. 8 And into whatsoever city ye enter, and they receive you, eat such things as are set before you: 9 and heal the sick that are therein, and say unto them, The kingdom of God is come nigh unto you. 10 But into whatsoever city ye shall enter, and they receive you not, go out into the streets thereof and say, 11 Even the dust from your city, that cleaveth to our

*feet, we wipe off against you: nevertheless know this, that the
kingdom of God is come nigh. 12 I say unto you, It shall be
more tolerable in that day for Sodom, than for that city.*

*17 And the seventy returned with joy, saying, Lord, even the
demons are subject unto us in thy name. 18 And he said unto
them, I beheld Satan fallen as lightning from heaven. 19
Behold, I have given you authority to tread upon serpents and
scorpions, and over all the power of the enemy: and nothing
shall in any wise hurt you. 20 Nevertheless in this rejoice not,
that the spirits are subject unto you; but rejoice that your names
are written in heaven.*

We read today that the story of the seventy – or the seventy-two,
depending on the source document from which our translation is
derived. Ancient scrolls are split about fifty-fifty on that score. But
regardless of the total number of disciples, many directives about how
we should evangelize are embedded in this story. Some are obvious,
some less so.

Obviously, we are supposed to travel and work in faith rather than
relying on material things. Thus, we are told to take no purse, wallet or
shoes. Rather than hopping from house to house, we're supposed to get
to know our hosts and become a part of the family for a while. He tells
us to eat what's put before us, something everyone in a family learns
from a young age – to respect and appreciate the food that hard work
has purchased, and love has seasoned.

And if the town doesn't welcome us? Well, the Lord says we should
wipe the dirt of their town from our feet and, on the way out, give
them the same message we always give whether we stay or whether we
go: the Kingdom of God is at hand, that is to say, it is right here and
within our reach if only we'll repent and believe in the Gospel. And
this isn't surprising, considering that Jesus says the law and the prophets
boil down to loving our neighbor as ourselves.

But what's less obvious is why the Lord twice refers to his disciples as laborers. Not as guests, teachers, or servants, but as laborers. A laborer sweats. His hands blister and his back aches. After years of toil his body can break down, and every day the chance of injury looms. So this is serious business to which we're being commissioned. This isn't tidying up and taking out the trash. Brothers and sisters, we're being called to hard labor, and we need to earn our keep.

Then, finally, the Lord says he has given us authority to tread upon snakes and scorpions and that nothing will harm us. Now this is a little sticky. We know that we shouldn't tempt God by throwing ourselves from high places expecting to fly, for example, and he's clear that we shouldn't celebrate victories over snakes and scorpions as our own. He says, "rejoice not, that the spirits are subject unto you; but rejoice that your names are written in heaven." What are we to make of this? Surely, we shouldn't expect immunity to suffering at the hands of risks and dangers of all kinds?

The lives of the saints and martyrs demonstrate that the most dedicated, pious, and selfless Christians suffer every pain, suffering, disease, injury, and injustice imaginable, every persecution, torture, and wrongdoing that can be conceived by evil forces and perpetrated by misguided people. So, perhaps Jesus is saying to us that just as we are sent out as a group we won't be overcome as a group. One or two of us might be taken out, but not all of us. Some of us may suffer horribly, but not all of us. An entire generation of disciples may perish, but the next generation will take up the labor anew.

Brothers and sisters, I think the Lord is sending us out into the world, not as individuals but as part of the immortal body of Christ. If that's what Jesus means, then we can all see that's true beyond doubt. Nothing to date has been successful halting the mission, and nothing ever will.

15th Sunday of Ordinary Time, July 10, 2022

Readings: Dt 30:10-14, Ps 69:14, 17, 30-31, 33-34, 36, 37, Col1:15-20, Lk 10:25-37

<u>Lk 10:25-37 World English Bible Catholic Edition</u>

25 Behold, a certain lawyer stood up and tested him, saying, "Teacher, what shall I do to inherit eternal life?"

26 He said to him, "What is written in the law? How do you read it?"

27 He answered, "You shall love the Lord your God with all your heart, with all your soul, with all your strength, and with all your mind; and your neighbor as yourself."

28 He said to him, "You have answered correctly. Do this, and you will live."

29 But he, desiring to justify himself, asked Jesus, "Who is my neighbor?"

30 Jesus answered, "A certain man was going down from Jerusalem to Jericho, and he fell among robbers, who both stripped him and beat him, and departed, leaving him half dead. 31 By chance a certain priest was going down that way.

When he saw him, he passed by on the other side. 32 In the same way a Levite also, when he came to the place and saw him, passed by on the other side. 33 But a certain Samaritan, as he traveled, came where he was. When he saw him, he was moved with compassion, 34 came to him, and bound up his wounds, pouring on oil and wine. He set him on his own animal, brought him to an inn, and took care of him. 35 On the next day, when he departed, he took out two denarii, gave them to the host, and said to him, 'Take care of him. Whatever you spend beyond that, I will repay you when I return.' 36 Now which of these three do you think seemed to be a neighbor to him who fell among the robbers?"

37 He said, "He who showed mercy on him."

Then Jesus said to him, "Go and do likewise."

Some years ago my friend and fellow fitness enthusiast Leo – a patron of St. Barachiel Chapel, a missionary to prisoners, and a powerful witness of the Gospel – shared with me an essay called "Iron and the Soul" by the famous punk rock star Henry Rollins. In the essay Rollins tells the story of his childhood rescue by a teacher named Mr. Pepperman. Rollins had been abandoned, bullied, and demeaned for most of his young life, so much so that by the time he was in high school he was possessed by fear, humiliation, self-loathing, and thoughts of suicide. But Mr. Pepperman intervened and saved his life. Leading by example, Pepperman showed him how to walk through the world in a different way, and he improved Rollin's health and self-esteem through weightlifting.

To be clear, Rollins is no saint, nor is he a Christian. But in the world of rock music, permeated with dissolution, drug and alcohol abuse, he sets a powerful example of sobriety, health, and fitness. A passionate advocate of peace and justice, Rollins doesn't fully realize how deeply Christian his viewpoint is. As an example, he says that most weightlifting injuries come from ego – lack of self-control and showing off – and that ego must be put aside in order to pursue real strength, both physical and internal. In his view, being pumped up with big muscles doesn't equate to strength, and training for cosmetic reasons is like doing good for the sake of appearances rather than out of sincerity. Real strength of character, he says, is manifested in kindness and understanding. Isn't that remarkable? I pray, and I hope you'll pray with me brothers and sisters, that Henry Rollins will one day put down the burden of his agnosticism, lift up the cross of Jesus Christ, and carry it in his heart. That would be the truest weight he ever lifted.

And so, when I read the story of the Good Samaritan, I think of Rollin's article for two reasons. The first and most obvious reason is, of course, that Mr. Pepperman is an example of a good Samaritan. He stepped in and gave young Henry Rollins the extra attention and mentorship he needed during a critical time. And by doing so, he saved a young man's mental, emotional, moral, and literal life.

The second, less obvious reason is that the parable of the Good Samaritan is just like iron, and iron doesn't lie. As Rollins points out in his article, in a world full of chaos and unpredictability, two hundred pounds of iron is always two hundred pounds of iron. You can either lift it or you cannot. If you lifted it last month and today you cannot, you've grown weaker. If you could not lift it last month and today you can, you've grown stronger. With iron there is no faking it. There are no excuses.

And that is the way it is with the parable of the Good Samaritan. We either lift up our neighbors or we do not. We can either be like a certain lawyer and argue about definitions and semantics, or we can pick up those who are in need of love, compassion, help, and protection and carry them to safety. We either bless those who curse us and do good to those who hate us, or we do not.

There is no faking it. There are no excuses.

16th Sunday of Ordinary Time, July 17, 2022

Readings: Gn 18:1-10a, Ps 15:2-3, 3-4, 5, Col 1:24-28, Lk 10:38-42

<u>Lk 10:25-37 World English Bible Catholic Edition</u>

38 As they went on their way, he entered into a certain village, and a certain woman named Martha received him into her house. 39 She had a sister called Mary, who also sat at Jesus' feet and heard his word. 40 But Martha was distracted with much serving, and she came up to him, and said, "Lord, don't you care that my sister left me to serve alone? Ask her therefore to help me."

41 Jesus answered her, "Martha, Martha, you are anxious and troubled about many things, 42 but one thing is needed. Mary has chosen the good part, which will not be taken away from her."

Isn't it miraculous, brothers and sisters, how much meaning is packed into the stories of Jesus life and works? In this short anecdote from Luke 10, barely a hundred words in length, there so many messages for us.

Historically and prophetically, this passage shows that Jesus knew he wasn't long for the world. He supports and justifies Mary shirking her chores to take advantage of receiving his teaching while there's still time. And he encourages Martha to do the same. We can imagine, can't we, after Jesus' crucifixion, Martha ends up wishing she has been a good deal more like Mary! And this is also a warning to humanity, isn't it? That we should all take the time to sit down at the feet of the Lord, Master and Savior Jesus Christ while we have time? For time is surely running out for each and every one of us to repent and believe in the Gospel before we go to our graves. And that's a powerful message for sure.

But what I most want to focus on in today's reading is its message of interiority and anti-materialism. When Martha is frustrated about Mary not helping with the chores, she asks Jesus to make her help. Isn't that the way it always is? For some people life is just easier. I know people like that. Money just seems to fall from the sky, good fortune follows them, they don't need to prepare or to struggle. And it's easy to be jealous like Martha, isn't it? We want them to have to struggle as hard as we do. We want the world to take them down a notch. But Jesus says that we shouldn't see things that way.

Jesus says, *"Martha, Martha, you are anxious and troubled about many things, but one thing is needed. Mary has chosen the good part, which will not be taken away from her."* He seems to be saying that there are many things that we have to do in our workaday lives. We have to do our chores, and make a living, and pay our bills, and take out the trash. We have to worry about our personal appearance, and we have to keep up appearances – we have to entertain our bosses, and host parties and holidays, and so on. We have to worry about money, and retirement, all of that. The list of things we have to be worried about is endless.

But in the end, only one thing is truly essential: that we listen to the teaching of the Lord. Because when we listen to his teachings, it directs how we do all of those other things. When we put the world second and really sit at the feet of the Lord, all of those other activities are redefined and properly ordered by his needs.

And therefore, although we are faulty and imperfect, we can at least fulfill all of our ever-multiplying obligations in the most Christ-like manner possible.

18th Sunday of Ordinary Time, July 29, 2022

Readings: Ecc 1:2; 2:21-23, Ps 90:3-4, 5-6, 12-13, 14 and 17, Col 3:1-5, 9-11, Lk 12:13-21

<u>Luke 12:13-21 World English Bible Catholic Edition</u>

13 One of the multitude said to him, "Teacher, tell my brother to divide the inheritance with me."

14 But he said to him, "Man, who made me a judge or an arbitrator over you?" 15 He said to them, "Beware! Keep yourselves from covetousness, for a man's life doesn't consist of the abundance of the things which he possesses."

16 He spoke a parable to them, saying, "The ground of a certain rich man produced abundantly. 17 He reasoned within himself, saying, 'What will I do, because I don't have room to store my crops?' 18 He said, 'This is what I will do. I will pull down my barns, build bigger ones, and there I will store all my grain and my goods. 19 I will tell my soul, "Soul, you have many goods laid up for many years. Take your ease, eat, drink, and be merry."'

20 "But God said to him, 'You foolish one, tonight your soul is required of you. The things which you have prepared—whose

will they be?' 21 So is he who lays up treasure for himself, and is not rich toward God."

I would like for us to explore together today, brothers and sisters, what Jesus might mean when he says in Luke12:14, *"Man, who made me a judge or an arbitrator over you?"* The question is, if we cannot rely on Jesus, our Lord, Master and Savior to adjudicate for us, upon whom can we rely? Why would Jesus, who comes "to judge the quick and the dead" as it says in the Apostle's Creed, deny his mandate to judge?

Often when exploring scripture, we find that context, as the saying goes, is king. So let's look at the stanzas immediately following. Jesus says, *"Beware! Keep yourselves from covetousness, for a man's life doesn't consist of the abundance of the things which he possesses."*

Perhaps, my friends, we are meant to understand that Jesus' judgement has nothing to do with the material world. His judgement is a form of heavenly judgement rather than a material one. Jesus, who is from heaven and of heaven, is concerned with heavenly things. What are heavenly things? Heavenly things, in Greek *epouranios* (ep-oo-RAN-ee-os) literally "of heaven," are the things that are in, of, or from the divine, eternal, spiritual world, or which relate to spiritual truths. Some examples:

- In John 3, when Nicodemus asks Jesus, "How can a man be born when he is old? Can he enter a second time into his mother's womb and be born?" Jesus answered, "That which is born of the flesh is flesh...Are you the teacher of Israel, and don't understand these things? ...If I told you earthly things and you don't believe, how will you believe if I tell you heavenly things?"
- In Hebrews 8, we read that the Tabernacle is an imperfect copy of the perfect heavenly sanctuary which contains

"heavenly things."
- In Genesis 1 we read, "God created man in his own image." We are imperfect material "earthly things" that are copies of the one, original, and perfect "heavenly thing."

In a similar way, an earthly judge is an imperfect image of the perfect heavenly judge, Jesus. An earthly judge sits in judgement of earthly matters, like the inheritance case the man posed to Jesus in today's reading. Jesus, on the other hand, sits in judgement of heavenly matters – the concerns of the spirit, our unseen thoughts and desires, our actual soul. He judges the degree of sin and disorder in our hearts – the covetousness itself – not the particulars of earthly cases regarding possessions.

If I'm correct, what this means is that Jesus has no interest in worldly squabbles. His courtroom is the human heart.

19th Sunday of Ordinary Time, August 7, 2022

Readings: Wis 18:6-9, Ps 33:1, 12, 18-19, 20-22, Heb 11:1-2, 8-19, Lk 12:32-48

<u>Luke 12:32-48 World English Bible Catholic Edition</u>

32 *"Don't be afraid, little flock, for it is your Father's good pleasure to give you the Kingdom. 33 Sell what you have and give gifts to the needy. Make for yourselves purses which don't grow old, a treasure in the heavens that doesn't fail, where no thief approaches and no moth destroys. 34 For where your treasure is, there will your heart be also.*

35 *"Let your waist be dressed and your lamps burning. 36 Be like men watching for their lord when he returns from the wedding feast, that when he comes and knocks, they may immediately open to him. 37 Blessed are those servants whom the lord will find watching when he comes. Most certainly I tell you that he will dress himself, make them recline, and will come and serve them. 38 They will be blessed if he comes in the second or third watch and finds them so. 39 But know this, that if the master of the house had known in what hour the thief was coming, he would have watched and not allowed his house to be broken into. 40 Therefore be ready also, for the Son of Man is coming in an hour that you don't expect him."*

41 Peter said to him, "Lord, are you telling this parable to us, or to everybody?"

42 The Lord said, "Who then is the faithful and wise steward, whom his lord will set over his household, to give them their portion of food at the right times? 43 Blessed is that servant whom his lord will find doing so when he comes. 44 Truly I tell you that he will set him over all that he has. 45 But if that servant says in his heart, 'My lord delays his coming,' and begins to beat the menservants and the maidservants, and to eat and drink and to be drunken, 46 then the lord of that servant will come in a day when he isn't expecting him and in an hour that he doesn't know, and will cut him in two, and place his portion with the unfaithful. 47 That servant who knew his lord's will, and didn't prepare nor do what he wanted, will be beaten with many stripes, 48 but he who didn't know, and did things worthy of stripes, will be beaten with few stripes. To whomever much is given, of him will much be required; and to whom much was entrusted, of him more will be asked."

Brothers and sisters, perhaps you are like me and, from time to time, with no rhyme or reason, the reality of a particular biblical reading crashes down like a thunderbolt. Now, the Gospel is always real – I don't mean to imply otherwise – it's just that there are times when it seems Jesus is speaking directly to me as if physically in the room. That is what happened with this passage the other day.

A little background is in order. As I've shared with you before, I lost my faith as a young man and spent many years practicing various religions before I found my way back to Christ and heard the call to pursue the priesthood. In those days, the one constant in my life was martial arts. Although I practiced many faiths for all those years, martial arts were, for all practical purposes, my religion. And the symbol I selected to represent my martial arts club all those years ago was a winged hourglass. I still run that club. It's called Heritage Self-Defense, and its logo is still a winged hourglass.

When I originally picked it back in 2008, it was because I thought it was cool. I thought it meant, "live life to the fullest because time flies." And that's true as far as it goes. But it wasn't until later, when I found my way back to Christ, that I saw a deeper meaning. The hourglass, with it's two identical halves, represents the incarnation of Jesus Christ, Man and God coming together as One, breaking into human time. I thought I had made up a cool symbol for my club. But in reality, I had been fully in God's grasp even then. I didn't pick the symbol. *God picked the symbol for me.* God knew exactly where I was headed and he put a logo in my head that I wouldn't appreciate fully until I appreciated the mission of his beloved Son.

And then the other day, preparing to write today's homily, this passage broke in upon me. "It is your Father's good pleasure to give you the Kingdom." *It is!* It felt like Jesus was right there in the room. *It is! Not "it will be" or "it was" but "it is."* Before, I had always read this as something that would happen in the future. I thought Jesus was saying that, in the fullness of time, we might perhaps inherit his kingdom. But I saw that we've already been given the kingdom. Jesus, our Lord, has ascended into heaven and left the household for a while, just like the lord in the parable. And we, his faithful servants, are charged with taking care of his kingdom just as he would, until he comes back.

And now that winged hourglass means something more. Yes, indeed, time flies. And at any moment our Lord will come home. And we would be wise to remember, "To whomever much is given, of him will much be required; and to whom much was entrusted, of him more will be asked."

20th Sunday of Ordinary Time, August 14th, 2022

Readings: Jer 38:4-6, 8-10, Ps 40:2, 3, 4, 18, Heb 12:1-4, Lk 12:49-53

<u>Jeremiah 38:4-6, 8-10 World English Bible Catholic Edition</u>

4 Then the princes said to the king, "Please let this man be put to death, because he weakens the hands of the men of war who remain in this city, and the hands of all the people, in speaking such words to them; for this man doesn't seek the welfare of this people, but harm."

5 Zedekiah the king said, "Behold, he is in your hand; for the king can't do anything to oppose you."

6 Then they took Jeremiah and threw him into the dungeon of Malchijah the king's son, that was in the court of the guard. They let down Jeremiah with cords. In the dungeon there was no water, but mire; and Jeremiah sank in the mire.

8 Ebedmelech went out of the king's house, and spoke to the king, saying, 9 "My lord the king, these men have done evil in all that they have done to Jeremiah the prophet, whom they have cast into the dungeon. He is likely to die in the place where he is, because of the famine; for there is no more bread in the city."

10 Then the king commanded Ebedmelech the Ethiopian, saying, "Take from here thirty men with you, and take up Jeremiah the prophet out of the dungeon, before he dies."

Some translations of these passages, especially older ones, say that Jeremiah was thrown into a dungeon. But the literal word in the Hebrew is *habbor*, which means "pit, well, or cistern," and in the Latin Vulgate translation the word used is *lacum* which means "lake." The reason why it was previously translated as "dungeon" is that it didn't make any sense to throw a human being into a place where precious water is stored. We take it for granted, brothers and sisters, but in some places in the world today, where things are very much like they were in the time of Jeremiah, water is as precious as silver or more so. Literally life and death.

So when the old-timers read this passage they probably thought, "That's stupid. This must mean 'dungeon,' not 'cistern.'" But make no mistake, Jeremiah was thrown into a cistern. A cistern is an underground space for storing precious water, usually collected rainwater. In ancient times, especially in dry climates like the Middle East, they are and were very common. And from time to time they cease to be viable. Their walls crack and they leak. Animals fall in, drown, and foul the water. Metals, minerals, or other contaminants leach into the water from the surrounding stone. And when that happens, cisterns are only good for one thing – garbage pits. Archeologists love to find old wells and cisterns that have been used this way. They're treasure troves. That's why we read, *"In the dungeon there was no water, but mire; and Jeremiah sank in the mire."* Why would we expect to find water in a dungeon? That sentence makes no sense unless we substitute the word "cistern" for "dungeon."

The fact that it's a cistern used as a dump explains why, further on, Ebedmelech says Jeremiah is "likely to die in the place where he is, because of the famine; for there is no more bread in the city." Times are so tough in Jerusalem during the Babylonian siege that there's no garbage going into the abandoned cistern where Jeremiah has been cast down. Ebedmelech is saying, "if we don't get him out soon, he's going to starve to death because there aren't any fresh scraps getting thrown down for him to scavenge upon."

In the Bible, details like this matter. So what's so important about the fact that Jeremiah has been thrown into a cracked or despoiled cistern being used as a dump? Because, remember, Jeremiah has been sent by God to get the people to dig deeper, to tap into Heavenly Father's wellspring of living water. In Jeremiah 2:13, God speaks to Jeremiah and declares, "For my people have committed two evils: they have forsaken me, the spring of living waters, and cut out cisterns for themselves: broken cisterns that can't hold water."

The crushing irony of the story, and the thunderous power of the prophesy, resounds through the ages! The people of Jerusalem, who are themselves broken cisterns for the living waters, threw the prophet who could save them into – what? A broken and despoiled cistern full of garbage.

Don't you see? Moses was cast into the water as a baby and rescued by a slave. Jeremiah was cast into the cistern and recued by the slave Ebedmelech. And, just like Moses and Jeremiah, we too are cast into the waters and rescued by a slave. Into the waters of baptism we go, and we are saved by Christ Jesus. For, as St. Paul said in Philippians 2: 5-7, Christ Jesus emptied himself, taking the form of a slave, being made in the likeness of men. My friends, let us not be broken cisterns, but rather fill ourselves up with the living waters of God.

22nd Sunday of Ordinary Time, August 28th, 2022

Readings: Sir 3:17-18, 20, 28-29, Ps 68:4-5, 6-7, 10-11, Heb 12:18-19, 22-24a, Lk 14:1, 7-14

Sirach 3:17-18, 20, 28-29 World English Bible Catholic Edition [1]

My son, go on with your business in humility;
so you will be loved by an acceptable man.
The greater you are, humble yourself the more,
and you will find favor before the Lord.
Don't seek things that are too hard for you,
and don't search out things that are above your strength.
The heart of the prudent will understand a proverb.
A wise man desires the ear of a listener.
Water will quench a flaming fire;
almsgiving will make atonement for sins.

Luke 14:1, 7-14 World English Bible Catholic Edition

When he went into the house of one of the rulers of the Pharisees on a Sabbath to eat bread, they were watching him.
7

He spoke a parable to those who were invited, when he noticed how they chose the best seats, and said to them, 8 "When you are invited by anyone to a wedding feast, don't sit in the best seat, since perhaps someone more honorable than you might be invited by him, 9 and he who invited both of you would come and tell you, 'Make room for this person.' Then you would begin, with shame, to take the lowest place. 10 But when you are invited, go and sit in the lowest place, so that when he who invited you comes, he may tell you, 'Friend, move up higher.' Then you will be honored in the presence of all who sit at the table with you. 11 For everyone who exalts himself will be humbled, and whoever humbles himself will be exalted."

12 He also said to the one who had invited him, "When you make a dinner or a supper, don't call your friends, nor your brothers, nor your kinsmen, nor rich neighbors, or perhaps they might also return the favor, and pay you back. 13 But when you make a feast, ask the poor, the maimed, the lame, or the blind; 14 and you will be blessed, because they don't have the resources to repay you. For you will be repaid in the resurrection of the righteous."

Brothers and sisters it's very hard to be humble when all day long, almost every message we receive from the culture, from the television, the internet, and social media says we should sing our own praises. "If you don't toot your own horn there will be no music." "Do your own thing." "Be your own person." "Live your best life" (as if there was more than one) and "Be your authentic self" (as if our authentic selves weren't childish brats who want dessert before the meal, fancy toys, and a life without homework, chores, or responsibilities.

The Book of Sirach says, "water quenches a flaming fire." I wonder though, why would we want to quench the flame of our pride? I mean, it's fun isn't it? It's great to enjoy the first seat at the table, am I right? It's fun to flaunt our trophies and certificates. It's perfectly natural to show off the things we bought with our hard-earned cash. We earned them, right? We worked hard for them didn't we?

Or did we?

Isn't it possible that we have them because others care deeply about us and taught us the skills and techniques we used to earn that trophy, award, or cash? Isn't it possible that we owe a debt of gratitude to others, maybe even some who have passed on, like our deceased parents or grandparents, our beloved mentor, coach, teacher, or bishop? Or maybe we owe your success to something we learned from a book whose author is long dead. Perhaps we owe something to the college where we earned our degree. Or to our spouses, family and friends, the ones who supported us physically and/or emotionally while we were struggling. There may even be some people we've forgotten that we owe because, when they gave us hard criticism, we preferred to part ways, only to realize later that they were right and we were wrong.

If we think hard about who deserves the credit for our successes, and if we take the time to cut up the pie of credit and serve it up, we may well find only a very small sliver left for ourselves. And maybe that last, tiny serving is attributable to good fortune or sheer luck. It's almost as if one could say, "to God alone be the glory."

We might also ask ourselves these sorts of questions when we are not doing well, or when those around us are failing. How much of our failures do we blame on others? How many of the failures that surround us are attributable to our poor leadership or our poor example? Things at first blush or not always what they seem.

When we are feeling down, often this is because we've subconsciously realized that we are at fault for something. The good news is that, as we read in Sirach, "alms atone for sins." Bake a cake for the family next door, or casserole for the elderly widow down the block. Visit a sick relative or friend. Volunteer your time for a charity. Don't just write a check or click a box on the internet. Physically do something, that's far better. Let's clean out our attics and donate the goods to a charity. How about we go through our kitchens, pull out the best, most expensive and yummy stuff, and donate it to the food drive (not the old, expired stuff like we usually do, if we're being honest). Physical demonstrations of sacrifice and almsgiving are uplifting because they are real. Think about it this way. Maybe the person you are helping had something to do with your success. God's ways are a mystery.

You never know.

23rd Sunday of Ordinary Time, Sept. 4th, 2022

Readings: Wis 9:13-18b, Ps 90:3-4, 5-6, 12-13, 14 and 17, Phmn 9-10, 12-17, Lk 14:25-33

<u>Luke 14:25-33 World English Bible Catholic Edition</u>

25 Now great multitudes were going with him. He turned and said to them, 26 "If anyone comes to me, and doesn't disregard† his own father, mother, wife, children, brothers, and sisters, yes, and his own life also, he can't be my disciple. 27 Whoever doesn't bear his own cross and come after me, can't be my disciple. 28 For which of you, desiring to build a tower, doesn't first sit down and count the cost, to see if he has enough to complete it? 29 Or perhaps, when he has laid a foundation and isn't able to finish, everyone who sees begins to mock him, 30 saying, 'This man began to build and wasn't able to finish.' 31 Or what king, as he goes to encounter another king in war, will not sit down first and consider whether he is able with ten thousand to meet him who comes against him with twenty thousand? 32 Or else, while the other is yet a great way off, he sends an envoy and asks for conditions of peace. 33 So therefore, whoever of you who doesn't renounce all that he has, he can't be my disciple.

Sometimes, when Jesus sets the bar as high as he does in today's gospel reading, we tend to prevaricate and think ourselves around into a kind of relaxed complacence. You know what I mean. We say to ourselves, "Well, this is all metaphorical. Jesus doesn't want to destroy civilization by turning everyone into penniless, family-hating homeless people. Somebody's gotta have a job or there won't be any food, goods, art, music, or medicine." And so we politely put these hard – one might even say *terrifying* – words of Jesus into a pretty little box and file them away where they can't scare us anymore.

But listen everybody, that is wrong, wrong, wrong. We cannot do that. Jesus is very clear on this point. He wants us to do the math. He wants us to add up the costs associated with turning away from his instructions. As we are constructing ourselves and building out our lives, Jesus wants us to make the same sorts of calculations that a builder makes when calculating the costs of building a structure. As we are trying to figure what we are going to fight for, protect and defend, he wants us to make the same evaluations a king, president, or prime minister makes when considering war. Jesus wants us to take this very seriously indeed.

How seriously? So seriously that he says we should despise even our own lives, pick up our own crosses, and follow him, or else we can't be his disciples.

Pick up our own cross?

Pick up our own cross.

Weigh that in your mind. Do the math. Fortunately, our government doesn't publicly execute criminals in the most humiliating and painful manner ever conceived. Fortunately, we no longer make criminals carry the instrument of their own execution to the killing ground, then nail them up so that passersby can jeer at them and watch them slowly die. Fortunately, we've never seen such a thing. But when Jesus was speaking the words in today's reading, everyone in earshot had witnessed the horrors of crucifixion. They knew exactly what he was asking. And so should we.

See here. There are so many demands on our time. Family members demand their share of our time and attention. Our bosses make additional demands on our time and are always rearranging our priorities. Plus we face financial demands – paying bills, taxes, loans, and all of that. Sometimes we can't even make ends meet. Our bodies make demands. It wants sleep, food, intimacy, entertainment, recreation, and all of that. And we face moral demands. Our political parties want us to toe the party line even when we disagree with elements of the platform. Our governments sometimes ask us to choose one of two reprehensible candidates. In the face of all these demands and compromises, day in and day out, we wonder:

Who am I? What am I doing? What's the point of all this?

Jesus *has* the answer and *is* the answer. When we value him most highly – mind, body, and soul; when we make him the landmark toward which we relentlessly march – as unwaveringly as possible – we have a mission, a direction, a role model, a king, and a purpose. Everything falls in line behind and beneath Jesus.

Can putting decency and morality ahead of family ties feel like "hate?" Sure it can. Can the stresses, setbacks, and sufferings of life can seem like dying a slow death? Of course. Can giving up the rat race, no longer trying to "keep up with the Jones'" and shrugging off the tyranny of material possessions feel like living the life of a wandering disciple? You bet. But do it we must.

If we do not, we will be as incomplete as the unfinished tower and we will lose the war against the wickedness and snares of the devil.

† *or, hate*

24th Sunday of Ordinary Time, Sept. 11th, 2022

Readings: Ex 32:7-11, 13-14, Ps 51:3-4, 12-13, 17, 19, 1 Tm 1:12-17, Lk 15:1-32

Luke 14:25-33 World English Bible Catholic Edition

1 Now all the tax collectors and sinners were coming close to him to hear him. 2 The Pharisees and the scribes murmured, saying, "This man welcomes sinners, and eats with them."

3 He told them this parable: 4 "Which of you men, if you had one hundred sheep and lost one of them, wouldn't leave the ninety-nine in the wilderness and go after the one that was lost, until he found it? 5 When he has found it, he carries it on his shoulders, rejoicing. 6 When he comes home, he calls together his friends and his neighbors, saying to them, 'Rejoice with me, for I have found my sheep which was lost!' 7 I tell you that even so there will be more joy in heaven over one sinner who repents, than over ninety-nine righteous people who need no repentance.

8 "Or what woman, if she had ten drachma coins, if she lost one drachma coin, wouldn't light a lamp, sweep the house, and seek diligently until she found it? 9 When she has found it, she calls together her friends and neighbors, saying, 'Rejoice with* *me, for I have found the drachma which I had lost!' 10 Even so, I tell you, there is joy in the presence of the angels of God over one sinner repenting."*

11 He said, "A certain man had two sons. 12 The younger of them said to his father, 'Father, give me my share of your property.' So he divided his livelihood between them. 13 Not many days after, the younger son gathered all of this together and traveled into a far country. There he wasted his property with riotous living. 14 When he had spent all of it, there arose a severe famine in that country, and he began to be in need. 15 He went and joined himself to one of the citizens of that country, and he sent him into his fields to feed pigs. 16 He wanted to fill his belly with the pods that the pigs ate, but no one gave him any. 17 But when he came to himself, he said, 'How many hired servants of my father's have bread enough to spare, and I'm dying with hunger! 18 I will get up and go to my father, and will tell him, "Father, I have sinned against heaven and in your sight. 19 I am no more worthy to be called your son. Make me as one of your hired servants."'

20 "He arose and came to his father. But while he was still far off, his father saw him and was moved with compassion, and ran, fell on his neck, and kissed him. 21 The son said to him, 'Father, I have sinned against heaven and in your sight. I am no longer worthy to be called your son.'

22 "But the father said to his servants, 'Bring out the best robe and put it on him. Put a ring on his hand and sandals on his feet. 23 Bring the fattened calf, kill it, and let's eat and celebrate; 24 for this, my son, was dead and is alive again. He was lost and is found.' Then they began to celebrate.

25 "Now his elder son was in the field. As he came near to the house, he heard music and dancing. 26 He called one of the servants to him and asked what was going on. 27 He said to him, 'Your brother has come, and your father has killed the fattened calf, because he has received him back safe and healthy.' 28 But he was angry and would not go in. Therefore his father came out and begged him. 29 But he answered his father, 'Behold, these many years I have served you, and I never disobeyed a commandment of yours, but you never gave me a goat, that I might celebrate with my friends. 30 But when this your son came, who has devoured your living with prostitutes, you killed the fattened calf for him.'

31 "He said to him, 'Son, you are always with me, and all that is mine is yours. 32 But it was appropriate to celebrate and be glad, for this, your brother, was dead, and is alive again. He was lost, and is found.' "

Brothers and sisters, in today's Gospel reading, the obvious messages sing out to us from the story of the prodigal son. We see that Jesus is speaking to the Pharisees, warning them not to be like the older son who resents the repentant, younger son. And he is also giving the Pharisees another message that he hopes they will appreciate, perhaps even more fully after his death and resurrection, which is that it's never too late to change direction and return to our Father in Heaven.

And we also easily see that Jesus was also speaking directly to everyone surrounding him at that time, just as he is speaking to each of us right now, and to everyone who ever reads this amazing parable, urging us not be afraid of our Heavenly Father's anger. But rather, when we come to ourselves and realize we have transgressed, we should go to him with a contrite heart and with true repentance just as the prodigal son did, and beg for forgiveness.

All of this is obvious. But what's less obvious is that Jesus is telling us to be wasteful with our possessions and our love. In the parable, the younger son is wasteful with his inheritance, and father's response to his son's sincere repentance is to be wasteful in kind – with love, food, and material gifts. Jesus wants us to freely forgive, to welcome home all those who, with truly remorseful hearts, return home after having been lost to sin and disobedience in the lands of godlessness. *Prodigal* actually means "wasteful" and "extravagant." So let us all be prodigal fathers and mothers, brothers and sisters, cousins and neighbors, who give away our love, attention and forbearance without strings, to all who sincerely repent.

And we'll be wise to remember that it was very hard for the prodigal son to admit his errors and go home. He was so low, so crushed by the guilt of his missteps, that he was deemed unworthy even to eat the food given to pigs. It is very hard for people to repent their ways, for some people, almost impossible. It's helpful to be mindful of the huge gulf that lies between shamefulness and recklessness.

Let us have patience and hope – for those who are still wandering, as well as for ourselves when we stumble – that our Father in heaven will celebrate and rejoice because we have been "dead and will come to life again."

25th Sunday of Ordinary Time, Sept. 18th, 2022

Readings: Am 8:4-7, Ps 113:1-2, 4-6, 7-8, 1 Tm 2:1-8, Lk 16:1-13

<u>Luke 16: 1-13 World English Bible Catholic Edition</u>

1 He also said to his disciples, "There was a certain rich man who had a manager. An accusation was made to him that this man was wasting his possessions. 2 He called him, and said to him, 'What is this that I hear about you? Give an accounting of your management, for you can no longer be manager.'

3 "The manager said within himself, 'What will I do, seeing that my lord is taking away the management position from me? I don't have strength to dig. I am ashamed to beg. 4 I know what I will do, so that when I am removed from management, they may receive me into their houses.' 5 Calling each one of his lord's debtors to him, he said to the first, 'How much do you owe to my lord?' 6 He said, 'A hundred batos of oil.' He said to him, 'Take your bill, and sit down quickly and write fifty.' 7 Then he said to another, 'How much do you owe?' He said, 'A hundred cors† of wheat.' He said to him, 'Take your bill, and write eighty.'*

8 "His lord commended the dishonest manager because he had done wisely, for the children of this world are, in their own generation, wiser than the children of the light. 9 I tell you, make for yourselves friends by means of unrighteous mammon, so that when you fail, they may receive you into the eternal tents. 10 He who is faithful in a very little is faithful also in much. He who is dishonest in a very little is also dishonest in much. 11 If therefore you have not been faithful in the unrighteous mammon, who will commit to your trust the true riches? 12 If you have not been faithful in that which is another's, who will give you that which is your own? 13 No servant can serve two masters, for either he will hate the one and love the other; or else he will hold to one and despise the other. You aren't able to serve God and Mammon."‡

Today's readings are very confusing at first glance. They seem to be coming at us from many different angles and proclaiming divergent messages, some of which seem to be at odds with Jesus' other teachings.

In the Amos reading, the prophet speaks out against rich merchants who can't wait to get religious obligations out of the way so that they can get back to profiteering. He rather angrily rails against rip-off artists who cheat the poor and put profits over people. But then, in the 1 Timothy reading, we are told to pray for everyone without anger or argument, because God wills everyone to be saved. Is anger justified or unjustified? Let's be clear, these are not at odds with each other. The goal of Amos is to forcefully confront the rich in the hopes that they will repent, change their ways, and be saved. And that is the hope for which the author of Timothy would have us pray.

With that apparent conflict resolved, let's see what can do about the ones apparent in Luke 16. Here Jesus tells us a story about money management. Now, why would he do this when, in many other places, he tells us to sell everything we have, give it to the poor, and follow him? Because his messages of total poverty are meant for his apostles, his inner circle. But this parable is being delivered to his disciples – everyday folks who want to follow his teachings.

And so he tells them the story of a steward (what today we'd call a business manager who works for an owner) who is accused of mismanagement, or perhaps embezzlement, probably the same behaviors Amos condemned in our first reading. Knowing he's about to be found out and fired, the dishonest steward starts making things right – revaluing purchases and writing down the debts he has inflated – in the hopes that he can make a few friends who'll support him when he's unemployed. His master praises him for trying to make good, even if it is only for his own benefit. Then, incredibly, Jesus tells us to be like the dishonest steward. He tells us Christians to be at least as wise with our money as the children of this world, to use it to make friends and so on.

If the master in this parable represents our Heavenly Father, and I think he does, the message here is that we cannot serve both God and our own needs. We must align our interests, even our finances, with the will of God as best we can. Jesus knows that worldly riches – he calls them "unrighteous mammon" – by their very nature, put us on the path to greed and avarice. But dealing with money is part of being in the world. And if we can't be trusted with worldly riches, which so often lead to dishonesty, how can we hope to be trusted with the true riches of the kingdom? Jesus leaves open the question of whether or not the master ultimately fires or retains the steward, a fascinating detail, the implication being that our fate with regard to God's judgement also remains an open question.

So let us be careful and unconflicted in the ordering of our desires, even our desire for prosperity, in accordance with God's will.

* 16:6 100 batos is about 395 liters or 104 U. S. gallons.

† 16:7 100 cors = about 2,110 liters or 600 bushels.

‡ 16:13 "Mammon" refers to riches or a false god of wealth.

26th Sunday of Ordinary Time, Sept. 25th, 2022

Readings: Am 6:1a, 4-7, Ps 146:7, 8-9, 9-10, 1 Tm 6:11-16, Lk 16:19-31

<u>Luke 16: 19-31 World English Bible Catholic Edition</u>

19 "Now there was a certain rich man, and he was clothed in purple and fine linen, living in luxury every day. 20 A certain beggar, named Lazarus, was taken to his gate, full of sores, 21 and desiring to be fed with the crumbs that fell from the rich man's table. Yes, even the dogs came and licked his sores. 22 The beggar died, and he was carried away by the angels to Abraham's bosom. The rich man also died and was buried. 23 In Hades, † he lifted up his eyes, being in torment, and saw Abraham far off, and Lazarus at his bosom. 24 He cried and said, 'Father Abraham, have mercy on me, and send Lazarus, that he may dip the tip of his finger in water and cool my tongue! For I am in anguish in this flame.'

25 "But Abraham said, 'Son, remember that you, in your lifetime, received your good things, and Lazarus, in the same way, bad things. But here he is now comforted and you are in anguish. 26 Besides all this, between us and you there is a great gulf fixed, that those who want to pass from here to you are not able, and that no one may cross over from there to us.'

27 "He said, 'I ask you therefore, father, that you would send him to my father's house— 28 for I have five brothers—that he may testify to them, so they won't also come into this place of torment.'

29 "But Abraham said to him, 'They have Moses and the prophets. Let them listen to them.'

30 "He said, 'No, father Abraham, but if one goes to them from the dead, they will repent.'

31 "He said to him, 'If they don't listen to Moses and the prophets, neither will they be persuaded if one rises from the dead.'"

In today's gospel reading, a rich man walks right past the poor, sick man Lazarus and offers no help. Both die. In the afterlife, Lazarus is raised into the life to come, while the rich man goes to the place of torment. Between them lies an inseparable gulf. What is this gulf? Certainly, it represents the gulf between those who do and do not trust in Jesus Christ! But this is a parable, and parables have infinite interpretations. And I'd like to suggest that the inseparable gulf in this parable represents the gulf of materialism, and that we can apply its lesson to the modern world.

There is a particularly insidious kind of death creeping through our communities these days. It strikes down even the wealthy, well-fed, and otherwise healthy. It's called *meaninglessness*. Despite the fact that there are fewer people living in poverty today than there have ever been in human history, there is an ongoing epidemic of meaninglessness.

Meaningless is spiritual death.

The Centers for Disease Control and Prevention reported in 2018 that suicide is up in the United states by 25% since 1999. A recent study in the UK found that 80% of those surveyed said their lives were meaningless. To quote behavioral scientist Clay Routledge, "We are a species that strives not just for survival, but also for significance. We want lives that matter. It is when people are not able to maintain meaning that they are most psychologically vulnerable. Empirical studies bear this out. A felt lack of meaning in one's life has been linked to alcohol and drug abuse, depression, anxiety and — yes —suicide. And when people experience loss, stress or trauma, it is those who believe that their lives have a purpose who are best able to cope with and recover from distress."[1]

In the parable, the rich man begs for relief from his torment. But what does he request? Does he ask for understanding? Does he repent and beg for a do-over? Does he ask what the difference is between him and Lazarus? No, he asks for Lazarus to bring a sip of water down to him. But Lazarus cannot come. There is no material thing, like a sip of water, that Lazarus can give to him that's going to work, because materialism isn't the answer. Modern culture is looking for meaning in a million sips of entertainment, fashion, money, sex, and science. But there is no meaning in these things.

Starting to understand, the rich man begs that Lazarus go to his family so that they'll change their ways. But he's still holding on to his materialist worldview. He still believes in evidence, and he thinks that if his family sees Lazarus, they'll change direction. But Abraham says no, they won't. If they see a man risen from the dead, they still won't believe. They won't trust their eyes.

This is true today. Dyed-in-the-wool materialists do not believe there is any meaning in miracles. Miracles are happening all around us every day, right now, and still people experiencing the affects of meaninglessness are searching for it in drugs, alcohol, medication, money, sex, and possessions. What they don't realize is that, just like

Lazarus in the parable, the meaning they seek can be found even when they have no possessions and no money. Even when they are at their absolute lowest, purpose and meaning are always available through faith in Jesus Christ, through whom they may be given to experience and share the true wealth of love, compassion, empathy, charity, humility, and devotion.

† 16:23 or, Hell

[1] Clay Routledge, "Suicides Have Increased. Is This an Existential Crisis?" *The New York Times*, June 2018, Retrieved from https://www.nytimes.com/2018/06/23/opinion/sunday/suicide-rate-existential-crisis.html

27th Sunday of Ordinary Time, Oct. 2nd, 2022

Readings: Hab 1:2-3; 2:2-4, Ps 95:1-2, 6-7, 8-9, 2 Tm 1:6-8, 13-14, Lk 17:5-10

<u>Luke 17: 5-10 World English Bible Catholic Edition</u>

5 The apostles said to the Lord, "Increase our faith."

6 The Lord said, "If you had faith like a grain of mustard seed, you would tell this sycamore tree†, 'Be uprooted and be planted in the sea,' and it would obey you. 7 But who is there among you, having a servant plowing or keeping sheep, that will say when he comes in from the field, 'Come immediately and sit down at the table'? 8 Wouldn't he rather tell him, 'Prepare my supper, clothe yourself properly, and serve me while I eat and drink. Afterward you shall eat and drink'? 9 Does he thank that servant because he did the things that were commanded? I think not. 10 Even so you also, when you have done all the things that are commanded you, say, 'We are unworthy servants. We have done our duty.'"

Eat five servings of fruits and vegetables per day. Get eight hours sleep. Maintain a body mass index under 25. Limit yourself to two hours of screen time per day for mental health. Don't smoke. Get a minimum of twenty minutes of aerobic exercise twice per week for cardiovascular health. Brush and floss twice per day. How many of us heed *all* of that advice? What's the problem? Don't we trust the scientific evidence?

Evidence shows that people who go to church live longer lives than those who don't. People who pray suffer from fewer mental health issues than those who don't. Churches promote diversity and reduce political polarization by bringing together people of vastly different races, ages, and political affiliations. Churchgoers donate more to charity, are more engaged in community activities, and volunteer more. And yet every day in the U.S. about five churches shut their doors forever. What's the problem? Do we not trust the evidence? ‡

Brothers and sisters, in the scene just prior to today's reading, Jesus tells his apostles, "If your brother sins against you seven times in the day, and seven times returns, saying, 'I repent,' forgive him." And the apostles say, "Increase our faith." The apostles are right there, observing Jesus' works, seeing the miracles, listening to his interpretations of scripture, and all of that. They know he's who he says he is. And yet they say, "Increase our faith." What's their problem? Don't they trust the evidence?

Jesus says, "If you had faith like a mustard seed..." If you had faith like a mustard seed, a very tiny seed that grows into an enormous plant, "you would tell this mulberry tree to be uprooted and be planted in the sea and it would obey you." In other words, if our faith was capable of ever-increasing strength, we could do the impossible. We could forgive our repentant brother seven times seven times. We'd be able to love our neighbor as ourselves. Maybe we could even love our enemies.

Through the parable of the servant coming in from the field, Jesus warns us that following the commandments is the bare minimum. We shouldn't pat ourselves on the back because we didn't raise up any idols, swear, murder, steal, or commit adultery today. Let's not sit down at the banquet and celebrate the fact that we did the bare minimum. We should have faith that, like a mustard seed, grows ever larger and ever stronger. As we see the evidence mounting – as we witness the transforming power of baptism, feel the demons being cast out of our own hearts, see the power of our churches to transform communities, and all of that – our faith shouldn't just hold its own. It should grow and grow until it becomes capable of the impossible. Impossible forgiveness. Impossible charity. Impossible love.

† More likely a mulberry tree. According to the International Standard Bible Encyclopedia, this is the sik´a - mīn , (συκάμινος , *sukáminos*) the black mulberry tree (*Morus nigra*; Natural Order, *Urlicaceae*), known in Arabic as *tût shrâmî* , "the Damascus mulberry," a fine tree which grows to the height of 30 ft. It produces the dark blood-red mulberry juice referred to in 1 Macc 6:34 (μόρον , *moron*), "the blood of ... mulberries," which was shown to the elephants of the Syrians. The white mulberry, *M. alba* , has white and less juicy fruit, and it is cultivated largely for the sake of its leaves with which the silkworms of the Lebanon are fed. The tree in Luke 19:3 is the *Ficus sycomorus*, called the sycamore fig or the fig-mulberry because its leaves resemble the mulberry.

‡ For more detail watch my video "Ten Reasons Even Non-Believers Should Go to Church[1]" at https://youtu.be/sKw7ZfDQnSo or read Robert D. Putnam's important study, "What's So Darned Special about Church Friends?" (2012) *Altruism, Morality & Social Solidarity Forum, American Sociological Association*, Vol 3 Issue 3, pp 19-21, Retrieved from https://wcfia.harvard.edu/files/wcfia/files/rputnam_church_friends.pdf

---

28th Sunday of Ordinary Time, Oct. 9th, 2022

Readings: 2 Kgs 5:14-17, Ps 98:1, 2-3, 3-4, 2 Tm 2:8-13, Lk 17:11-19

<u>2 Kings 5:14-17 World English Bible Catholic Edition</u>

14 Then went he down and dipped himself seven times in the Jordan, according to the saying of the man of God; and his flesh was restored like the flesh of a little child, and he was clean. 15 He returned to the man of God, he and all his company, and came, and stood before him; and he said, "See now, I know that there is no God in all the earth, but in Israel. Now therefore, please take a gift from your servant."

16 But he said, "As Yahweh lives, before whom I stand, I will receive none." He urged him to take it; but he refused. 17 Naaman said, "If not, then, please let two mules' load of earth be given to your servant; for your servant will from now on offer neither burnt offering nor sacrifice to other gods, but to Yahweh.

Wow, what a story! Naaman, a great general of the Syrian army has leprosy. More than likely this is psoriasis or eczema not leprosy – there's little evidence for leprosy being prevalent in that area at that time.

And a little slave girl from Israel working in the court of the king suggests he might be healed by Elisha. This little girl embodies the reality that very small but very potent ideas are able to infiltrate the halls of political power. They seem innocent and inconsequential, but they have incredible implications. She suggests this tiny idea called *faith*. It seems so innocent, doesn't it? Just try. Ask the prophet, do what he says, and see what happens.

So the king tells Naaman to take some gifts to Elisha and give it a shot. Can't hurt, right? So Naaman does, and Elisha tells him to do a simple thing – dip yourself seven times in the Jordan river. Ridiculous! So simple! Naaman gets steaming mad. He says the water in the Jordan is just like any other river. He says he could've stayed home and taken a dunk, this is baloney!

We Christians see this all the time. For two thousand years, we've been hearing this from people who question the reality of our faith. They can't bring themselves to hear the message of a little child who says, "have a little faith." It seems too simple, too basic, too infantile. In modern times it's the scientists and the academics. They say, it's ridiculous, that Christian myths are no different than the Greek myths, the Norse myths, the Hindu, Mayan, African, or the Aboriginal myths. The scientists say that you can't be healed by dipping yourself in a river.

Naaman's servants, just simple folks, people with no power and no authority, they set him straight. They suggest that if Elisha's instructions had been costly and extravagant he would've played along. So why not do it? Basically they say, "have a little faith."

And I'm saying the same thing as the little girl, the same thing as Naaman's servants. This simple idea called "faith," this tiny, unassuming Judeo-Christian innovation, transforms everything. It heals the spirit, it heals bodies, relationships, and even nations. An alcoholic named Bill Wilson's message of faith spawned Alcoholics Anonymous, the most effective anti-addiction treatment plan ever devised, and its faith-based methods have healed millions of addicts. When Pope John

Paul II preached to Poland in the 1980s and they listened, the sickness of communism was healed in that country and in the whole of Eastern Europe. When Rev. Dr. Martin Luther King Jr. preached to America and we listened, the wounds of segregation, fear, and hatred were healed. Billy Graham preached privately to twelve consecutive U.S. Presidents, and heaven knows what those leaders, and the world, would have been like without his messages.

And yet, despite this evidence, many people refuse to dip themselves in the river Jordan, to be baptized and transformed by faith. Not blind belief uninformed by evidence, but by faith born of trust.

The messages of Naaman's remarkable story are many and manifold. Fellow Christians, let us not make the mistake that Naaman made. Let's not cling to our pre-conversion idolatry by dragging along with us two mule-loads of baggage. And to those who are not Christians who can hear my voice: listen to the advice of a little girl and heed two thousand years of evidence.

Trust in the Lord. Dip yourself in the Jordan River. Be baptized, and be healed.

30th Sunday of Ordinary Time, Oct. 23rd, 2022

Readings: Sir 35:12-14, 16-18, Ps 34:2-3, 17-18, 19, 23, 2 Tm 4:6-8, 16-18, Lk 18:9-14

<u>Luke 18:9-14 World English Bible Catholic Edition</u>

9 He also spoke this parable to certain people who were convinced of their own righteousness, and who despised all others: 10 "Two men went up into the temple to pray; one was a Pharisee, and the other was a tax collector. 11 The Pharisee stood and prayed by himself like this: 'God, I thank you that I am not like the rest of men: extortionists, unrighteous, adulterers, or even like this tax collector. 12 I fast twice a week. I give tithes of all that I get.' 13 But the tax collector, standing far away, wouldn't even lift up his eyes to heaven, but beat his breast, saying, 'God, be merciful to me, a sinner!' 14 I tell you, this man went down to his house justified rather than the other; for everyone who exalts himself will be humbled, but he who humbles himself will be exalted."

"Lord Jesus Christ, Son of God, have mercy on me, a sinner." These immortal words of prayer from today's Gospel reading, echo up and down the centuries. In the Orthodox tradition, this is often called the

"Jesus Prayer," it is believed to be the unceasing prayer encouraged by St. Paul in 1 Thessalonians 5:17 ("Pray without ceasing"). It central to the ascetic Orthodox practice of both monks and lay people known as *hesychasm* or "stillness."

It is also esteemed in the Roman Catholic Church. According to Catechism 2667:

> *"This simple invocation of faith developed in the tradition of prayer under many forms in East and West. the most usual formulation, transmitted by the spiritual writers of the Sinai, Syria, and Mt. Athos, is the invocation, "Lord Jesus Christ, Son of God, have mercy on us sinners." It combines the Christological hymn of Philippians 2:6-11 with the cry of the publican and the blind men begging for light. By it the heart is opened to human wretchedness and the Savior's mercy."*

The Jesus Prayer also shows up in the Anglican Rosary, and is sometimes called "The Sinner's Prayer" by Evangelical Christians.

Why is it that these words have had such far-reaching, and long-lasting impact? What is it about this story – about the contrast between the Pharisee and the tax collector – that's so important? Perhaps it is because self-righteousness is so toxic and because humility, its opposite, is so powerful. Self-righteousness is toxic to our souls. When we begin to think that we've arrived, that we have no more work to do, our growth stops. When we begin to think that we are better than our neighbors, this is the slippery slope that begins with condescension and eventually ends in spite and hatred – the opposite of loving one's neighbor.

Self-righteousness is also poisonous to the spreading of our faith to the spiritually starved who are in want. The foremost complaint I hear about Christians in the course of my evangelization work is that Christians are self-righteous jerks. They say that we Christians think we have all the answers. They say that we think we are saved and everyone else is damned, and nobody wants to spend time with holier-than-thou braggarts. It's one thing to harm our own growth and development, but poisoning the well of evangelization compounds the sin.

Humility – the opposite of self-righteousness – has the opposite effect. Humility fuels the way of Christ. It powers our development and improves our evangelization efforts. This is why, when we say the Confiteor and confess our sins, we rap our breasts with our knuckles just as the tax collector beats his breast and begs for mercy. This confession and prayer for mercy is merely the beginning. It is a knock on the door of the heart so that humility can enter.

All Souls' Day (observed) Sunday, Oct. 30th, 2022

Readings: Rv 7:2-4, 9-14, 24:1bc-2, 3-4ab, 5-6, 1 Jn 3:1-3, Mt 5:1-12a

<u>Matthew 5:1-12a World English Bible Catholic Edition</u>

1 Seeing the multitudes, he went up onto the mountain. When he had sat down, his disciples came to him. 2 He opened his mouth and taught them, saying,

3 "Blessed are the poor in spirit,

for theirs is the Kingdom of Heaven.

4 Blessed are those who mourn,

for they shall be comforted.

5 Blessed are the gentle,

for they shall inherit the earth.

6 Blessed are those who hunger and thirst for righteousness,

for they shall be filled.

7 Blessed are the merciful,

for they shall obtain mercy.

8 Blessed are the pure in heart,

for they shall see God.

9 Blessed are the peacemakers,

for they shall be called children of God.

10 Blessed are those who have been persecuted for righteousness' sake,

for theirs is the Kingdom of Heaven.

11 "Blessed are you when people reproach you, persecute you, and say all kinds of evil against you falsely, for my sake. 12 Rejoice, and be exceedingly glad, for great is your reward in heaven.

Pawpaw, my maternal grandfather, was a pilot in WWII. He earned enough medals to fill a cigar box, one of which was a Distinguished Flying Cross for acts of heroism, bravery, and extraordinary gallantry under enemy fire. He was a great American and a fine grandfather.

My fondest memory of him dates back to when I was about twelve. My teenage uncle and I went off to explore Rattlesnake Creek and we didn't come back for lunch as we had promised. When we finally emerged from the woods, eight hours late and after dark, we found our entire family and two police officers standing in the yard. Illuminated by flashing red lights, they were discussing the need to call out the dogs. They converged on us, hopping mad. But, with outstretched arms, Pawpaw stood between us and the crowd. He wouldn't let anyone harass us. "Boys will be boys," he told them, then turned to us and said, "You two, go wash up and get ready for bed." And that was the end of it. No tongue-lashing, no punishment. He knew we knew better and would never do it again.

I also remember him taking me to McDonald's when I was about eight years old. After we ate, he put me on his lap so that I could drive his cherished Buick around the parking lot. I remember him giving me my first big-boy haircut. I remember him teaching me how to properly shine a pair of shoes before church. I recall him making everyone root beer floats after Sunday dinner. And I solemnly remember, in the summer of 1980, when he died from his fifth heart attack.

I mourned his loss, but some did not. Because, I regret to say, there was more to this man than warm memories. PawPaw returned from the war with what we now call PTSD. He got little sympathy and support from the community and armed forces and struggled alone. He was given to fits of depression, rage, and cruelty. I heard from relatives chilling tales of cold malice and wicked vengeance, some from my mother. She had borne the brunt of his struggles. But I never witnessed any of that firsthand. And so, while I mourned his loss, others did not. There are those who will tell you that the right place for him is hell.

Join with me, my friends, as I beg our Heavenly Father to find it in his heart to deliver him to heaven for the man he was when he was at his best rather than sending him to hell for his sins. Pray with me, brothers and sisters, for my grandfather and for all departed souls. For our heroes and departed loved ones, yes; but also for the baptized and the unbaptized, for those who died in repentance and those who died before they saw the light. I assure you, my friends, the good and the evil are often one and the same, like opposing sides of the same coin, and they desperately need our prayers.

We have all made mistakes and errors, and no man's fate is certain. Just as we would appreciate the prayers of our loved ones, let us then obey our Lord Jesus' instruction to do for others what we would have them do for us (Matt. 7:12). Let us pray together the prayer of Our Lady of Fatima: "Oh my Jesus, forgive us our sins, save us from the fires of hell, and lead all souls to heaven, especially those most in need of thy mercy."

32nd Sunday in Ordinary Time, Nov. 6th, 2022

Readings: 2 Mc 7:1-2, 9-14, Ps 17:1, 5-6, 8, 15, 2 Thes 2:16-3:5, Lk 20:27-38

<u>2 Maccabees 7:1-2, 9-14 World English Bible Catholic Edition</u>

1 It came to pass that seven brothers and their mother were at the king's command taken and shamefully handled with scourges and cords, to compel them to taste of the abominable swine's flesh. 2 One of them made himself the spokesman and said, "What would you ask and learn from us? For we are ready to die rather than transgress the laws of our ancestors."

9 When he was at the last gasp, he said, "You, miscreant, release us out of this present life, but the King of the world will raise us who have died for his laws up to an everlasting renewal of life."

10 After him, the third was made a victim of their mocking. When he was required, he quickly put out his tongue, and stretched out his hands courageously, 11 and nobly said, "I got these from heaven. For his laws' sake I treat these with contempt. From him, I hope to receive these back again." 12 As a result, the king himself and those who were with him were astonished at the young man's soul, for he regarded the pains as nothing.

13 When he too was dead, they shamefully handled and tortured the fourth in the same way. 14 Being near to death he said this: "It is good to die at the hands of men and look for the hope which is given by God, that we will be raised up again by him. For as for you, you will have no resurrection to life."

At 7:30 AM on the 16th of March, 1968 the soldiers of Company C, first Battalion, 20th Infantry, U.S. Army marched into My Lai, Vietnam and started killing everything that was walking, crawling, running, or growing – women, children, animals, and crops. It was hard work. It was hot. So after a few hours they took a break. While they sat in the shade and had some water and some rations, did anybody desert? Did anybody call HQ and report the tragedy? Nope. When they were rested up, they went back and started killing some more.

When we are tested, brothers and sisters, it might not be as easy as it was for the brothers in today's Old Testament reading. At least the bad guys were on the other side. What if your brothers aren't being tortured beside you? What if they are the ones doing the torturing? What if they're the ones telling you to break God's rules?

Warrant Officer Hugh Thompson Jr., aged just 25 years, a recon helicopter pilot, was flying air support when he noticed movement in a ditch full of civilian bodies. He assumed they were victims of enemy forces. He landed the 'copter and began to look for help rescuing survivors. One soldier told him he would only "help them out of their misery." Another told him he was "just following orders." He observed one of them shoot an unarmed woman at point blank range. Shocked, confused, and infuriated, Thompson radioed headquarters and reported what he witnessed.

Spotting a group of women, children, and old men in a bunker, Thompson landed his helicopter between them and approaching U.S. soldiers. Risking court martial and the real danger of friendly fire, he told his crew to fire on anyone who attacked the civilians while he was attempting rescue. Fortunately, that did not happen and a dozen innocents were flown to safety. They continued rescuing more non-combatants, including a 4-year-old girl they found unharmed, buried beneath the dead bodies of her fellow villagers.

Eventually a cease fire was ordered, but not until between 350 and 500 unarmed women, children, and elderly had been butchered. Then came the cover-up. Thompson was awarded the Distinguished Flying Cross, but the citation was filled with lies to hide the atrocities. So he threw it in the trash.

Friends, we don't do the right thing for the recognition of men – we do what's right to please God. God is steadfast. Men are fickle. So I'm sure you can predict what happened when the truth came out. Hugh Clowers Thompson Jr., former Boy Scout, devoted Episcopalian, and one of America's greatest heroes, was called a traitor by the media. Members of congress suggested he be court-martialed. He received death threats. Dead animals were left on his doorstep.

Eventually, after a four-year investigation, over 200 U.S. personnel were charged with crimes and/or court-martialed. Thompson faded from the public eye. After 20 years in the Army, he retired and became a private pilot. In 1998, 30 years to the day after the massacre, he and his courageous crew, Glenn Andreotta and Lawrence Colburn, were awarded the U.S. Army's highest award for bravery outside combat – the Soldier's Medal.

After great tribulation, Thompson's story ended well. But there's no assurance the same will be true when impossible moral choices are forced on us. We may well perish like the seven brothers. All we can do is try and prepare ourselves to stand our ground and remember that, even if things don't end well in this world, God is with us, and there is hope of life in the world to come.

33rd Sunday in Ordinary Time, Nov. 13th, 2022

Readings: Mal 3:19-20a, Ps 98:5-6, 7-8, 9, 2 Thes 3:7-12, Lk 21:5-19

<u>Luke 21:5-19 World English Bible Catholic Edition</u>

As some were talking about the temple and how it was decorated with beautiful stones and gifts, he said, 6 "As for these things which you see, the days will come in which there will not be left here one stone on another that will not be thrown down."

7 They asked him, "Teacher, so when will these things be? What is the sign that these things are about to happen?"

8 He said, "Watch out that you don't get led astray, for many will come in my name, saying, 'I am he†,' and, 'The time is at hand.' Therefore don't follow them. 9 When you hear of wars and disturbances, don't be terrified, for these things must happen first, but the end won't come immediately."

10 Then he said to them, "Nation will rise against nation, and kingdom against kingdom. 11 There will be great earthquakes, famines, and plagues in various places. There will be terrors and great signs from heaven. 12 But before all these things, they will lay their hands on you and will persecute you, delivering you up to synagogues and prisons, bringing you before kings and governors for my name's sake. 13 It will turn out as a testimony for you. 14 Settle it therefore in your hearts not to meditate beforehand how to answer, 15 for I will give you a mouth and wisdom which all your adversaries will not be able to withstand or to contradict. 16 You will be handed over even by parents, brothers, relatives, and friends. They will cause some of you to be put to death. 17 You will be hated by all men for my name's sake. 18 And not a hair of your head will perish.

19 "By your endurance you will win your lives."

Like the disciples in today's reading, we are always asking, "When? When, Lord, are you going to come in judgment and wipe away the old and establish a new heaven and a new Earth?" Many have there been, and many even now, who incessantly pour over the Bible searching for symbolic meanings and historical clues – and even apply mathematical formulas and obscure numerological fortune telling methods! – to try and discern when the end of days will come. Still more relentlessly search the Bible for proof that the prophetic words of Jesus are speaking of events in the past, such as the destruction of the temple in Jerusalem, the fall of the Roman Empire, World War Two, and so on. Those who look solely to the future or solely to the past are wide of the mark. They deeply underestimate the power of the Word and its prevailing place at the *center of reality.*

Listen to the words of Revelation 4:6b-8.

In the middle of the throne, and around the throne were four living creatures full of eyes before and behind. 7 The first creature was like a lion, the second creature like a calf, the third creature had a face like a man, and the fourth was like a flying *eagle. 8 The four living creatures, each one of them having six wings, are full of eyes around and within. They have no rest day and night, saying, "Holy, holy, holy* is the Lord God, the Almighty, who was and who is and who is to come!"*

"Who was, who is and is to come!" The eyes of the angels are in front, behind and within because they must penetrate all times and all places. Make no mistake, Jesus answered the disciples the way he did in today's reading, mixing the symbolic and the literal together, for a reason. When he spoke of the temple stones being cast down, was he speaking of his crucifixion? *Yes.* Was he speaking of the Temple of Jerusalem being destroyed? *Yes.* Was he telling us to be mindful of our own death? *Yes!* It's not either/or – *it is all three.* Were his apocalyptic words about the fall of Babylon? The fall of Rome? The possible collapse of the United States? World War I, World War II, the present war in Ukraine, or the possibility of World War III? *Yes!* He was speaking about all of this. Jesus spoke, will speak, and is speaking right now, directly to everyone in all places in all times. In Rev 13:8, he is "the Lamb slain from the foundation of the world." Our minds strain with the weight of it.

Christ died on a cross before the universe was made because he is not bound by the chains of time.

Jesus is the Truth that speaks to all people, in all places, and in all times! The words he spoke to the disciples in today's reading are eternally relevant! Whenever war, famine, and destruction break into our lives, as they always do, we mustn't be afraid or allow ourselves to be led astray by false teachers. We will be betrayed by governments, employers, neighbors, friends, even family and loved ones. There is always a coming persecution, because those who behave morally and ethically are always attacked and peer-pressured by misguided souls who resent those they label as "do-gooders." Betrayal, hatred, and slander are a persistent threat to anyone with a moral, ethical compass. We will always be hated by somebody because of Christ's name.

But here's the good news: the son of man is always "coming in a cloud with great glory." (Luke 21:27). When the newly-converted soul sees the truth of Christ for the first time, Jesus has come. When we conquer moments of fear and despair through prayer, Jesus has come! Have no fear. Do not prepare your defense beforehand. Christ came in the past, Christ is here now, and Christ will come in the future to any person who seeks his face. Not a hair on the head of one who follows him will be destroyed forever.

Because ours is the blessed hope of a new life in the world to come.

Solemnity of Our Lord Jesus Christ, King of the Universe, Nov. 20ᵗʰ, 2022

Readings: 2 Sm 5:1-3, Ps 122:1-2, 3-4, 4-5, Col 1:12-20, Lk 23:35-43

<u>Luke 23:35-43 World English Bible Catholic Edition</u>

The people stood watching. The rulers with them also scoffed at him, saying, "He saved others. Let him save himself, if this is the Christ of God, his chosen one!"

36 The soldiers also mocked him, coming to him and offering him vinegar, 37 and saying, "If you are the King of the Jews, save yourself!"

38 An inscription was also written over him in letters of Greek, Latin, and Hebrew: "THIS IS THE KING OF THE JEWS."

39 One of the criminals who was hanged insulted him, saying, "If you are the Christ, save yourself and us!"

40 But the other answered, and rebuking him said, "Don't you even fear God, seeing you are under the same condemnation? 41 And we indeed justly, for we receive the due reward for our deeds, but this man has done nothing wrong." 42 He said to Jesus, "Lord, remember me when you come into your Kingdom."

43 Jesus said to him, "Assuredly I tell you, today you will be with me in Paradise."

The first criminal says, "If you are the Christ, save yourself and us!" This man, a true materialist, was speaking only of bodies on crosses at that time and in that place. Today as then, there are billions of materialists like this. The equivalent person in the modern world is the atheist who says something like, "Jesus never saved anyone. If he wanted to save people, he would've come to Earth with antibiotics, electricity, and modern plumbing."

The materialist Jews of Christ's day wanted a warrior king to come and bring peace to Israel by liberating them from the oppression of Rome. The materialist of today wants peace through technology and government authority. As ever, the materialist is blind to the universal, metaphysical, healing power of Peace.

St. Paul said that Christ is, *"the image of the invisible God, the firstborn of all creation"* (Col 1:12-20) and *"all the fullness was pleased to dwell in him, and through him to reconcile all things to himself by him, whether things on the earth or things in the heavens, having made peace through the blood of his cross."* (Col 1:19-20).

What is this Peace that comes through acknowledging Christ as King? This is the Peace of acceptance that comes from faith and saves us from fear, anxiety, worry, and suffering. This is the Peace which is the absence of vengeful thoughts and actions that comes from understanding that judgement is in God's hands. This is the Peace that comes when we understand that God loves us so much that he came to earth and entered into our state of suffering beside us. His is the Peace that is the harmony existing between and among all those who understand that, as children of God, we are all brothers and sisters by blood – the blood of the cross.

The poor materialist on the cross who asked Christ to save his physical body from the immediate suffering of crucifixion could not see the potential in Christ's sacrifice, just as the modern-day materialist is blind to the billions of lives saved by the Peace of Christ – saved from war, saved from privation, starvation, and hardship by Christian charity, saved from self-harm and suicide, and indeed, saved from the death that lasts forever.

Christ is King, the Prince of Peace (Isaiah 9:6). Let us praise Him and rejoice in his saving Peace.

First Day of Advent, Nov. 27th, 2022

Readings: Is 2:1-5, Ps 122: 1-2, 3-4, 4-5, 6-7, 8-9, Rom 13:11-14, Mt 24:37-44

Matthew 24:37-44 World English Bible Catholic Edition

Jesus said to his disciples: "As the days of Noah were, so will the coming of the Son of Man be. 38 For as in those days which were before the flood they were eating and drinking, marrying and giving in marriage, until the day that Noah entered into the ship, 39 and they didn't know until the flood came and took them all away, so will the coming of the Son of Man be. 40 Then two men will be in the field: one will be taken and one will be left. 41 Two women will be grinding at the mill: one will be taken and one will be left. 42 Watch therefore, for you don't know in what hour your Lord comes. 43 But know this, that if the master of the house had known in what watch of the night the thief was coming, he would have watched, and would not have allowed his house to be broken into. 44 Therefore also be ready, for in an hour that you don't expect, the Son of Man will come."

Brothers and sisters, there's not a geologist in the world who won't tell you that floods swept the world after the last glacial period ended. That's why virtually every culture on earth has a flood myth. Many of the world's plants, animals, and people were wiped out by real floods in the distant past. So: did the biblical flood of Noah really happen? Sure. Maybe the particulars aren't exact, like the precise dimensions of the ark. No 300-cubit-long replica – that's over 500 feet! – of the ark has every successfully floated. That's because it is a fact of science that the practical size limit of a ship, due to the material limits of spliced wooden beams, is about half that. So what? The message is 100% true. The biblical flood happened. And there will be more literal floods in the future, both large and small. They're in the news every day.

But the flood was a spiritual flood too. Noah, a righteous man, was surrounded on every side by corruption, lawlessness, and immorality. He and his family were at very real risk of drowning in the waters of chaos and iniquity. But he sheltered his family from all of that. He showed them right from wrong. He explained to them the structure of the universe, taught them about God's creation, educated them about how God is the foundation of culture, morality, and science. Doesn't the story say that Noah built an impossibly large boat and brought into it pairs of every animal species and the seeds of every plant? What a metaphor for Noah's leadership! Noah represents the figure whose unified wisdom across many dimensions – in construction, science, law, education, parenting, and so on – is a storehouse of almost infinite potential. A leader like him can singlehandedly rebuild a ruined culture.

Here's the thing though: Jesus Christ is just like Noah, *only better*. Our Lord does this over and over again. The story of every biblical patriarch, from Adam down to David, is the story of an imperfect predecessor of Jesus Christ. Adam is the first man, but Jesus is first *perfect* Man. Moses is a great high priest, but Jesus is the *perfect* high priest. David is a great king, but Jesus Christ is a *perfect* King.

So yes, Jesus Christ is the perfect Noah. His knowledge of science and law is perfect because he is the creator of the universe and the architect of both existence and goodness. He has built for us an ark in the form of a church into which we can bring our families and our extended church families. In it we preserve our knowledge, our wisdom, and our faith against the flood of chaos and corruption threatening to drown the world around us. Yes indeed, Jesus Christ is the perfect Noah. He teaches us how to build our bodies, minds, and spirits into arks that can ride on the waves of decadence and evil and withstand the torrential rains of selfishness and tides of ignorance that are always and forever falling and rising around us.

Let us strive, as the children of Noah and Jesus Christ, to make ourselves and our churches into arks that can withstand the eternal floods of this world.

Second Sunday of Advent, Dec. 4th, 2022

Readings: Is 11:1-10, Ps 72:1-2, 7-8, 12-13, 17, Rom 15:4-9, Mt 3:1-12

<u>Matthew 3:1-12 World English Bible Catholic Edition</u>

1 In those days, John the Baptizer came, preaching in the wilderness of Judea, saying, 2 "Repent, for the Kingdom of Heaven is at hand!" 3 For this is he who was spoken of by Isaiah the prophet, saying,

"The voice of one crying in the wilderness,

make the way of the Lord ready!

Make his paths straight!"✡

4 Now John himself wore clothing made of camel's hair with a leather belt around his waist. His food was locusts and wild honey. 5 Then people from Jerusalem, all of Judea, and all the region around the Jordan went out to him. 6 They were baptized by him in the Jordan, confessing their sins.

7 But when he saw many of the Pharisees and Sadducees coming for his baptism, he said to them, "You offspring of vipers, who warned you to flee from the wrath to come? 8 Therefore produce fruit worthy of repentance! 9 Don't think to yourselves, 'We have Abraham for our father,' for I tell you that God is able to raise up children to Abraham from these stones. 10 Even now the ax lies at the root of the trees. Therefore every tree that doesn't produce good fruit is cut down, and cast into the fire.

11 "I indeed baptize you in water for repentance, but he who comes after me is mightier than I, whose sandals I am not worthy to carry. He will baptize you in the Holy Spirit. 12 His winnowing fork is in his hand, and he will thoroughly cleanse his threshing floor. He will gather his wheat into the barn, but the chaff he will burn up with unquenchable fire."*

✡ 3:3 Isaiah 40:3

Surviving in the desert alone makes even the most hardened survival experts quake in their boots. The level of precision, calmness, discipline, and wisdom that it takes to survive alone in the desert – the most forsaken environment on earth – is staggering. The landscape is dizzyingly desolate. There are no landmarks you can use to find your way. And getting lost is doubly dangerous there, because nourishment and water are both incredibly scarce. Every step you take, every calorie of energy you burn and teaspoon of water you lose through perspiration, could be the difference between life and death. I once spent several days at a survival school in the high deserts of Utah. There were three dozen people in the camp and several survival instructors there. Even so, I felt raw, exposed, and in real danger.

So what kind of man is this John the Baptist, this prophet wearing skins of camel hide, surviving on locusts and honey? He's wearing camel hide because the camel, one of the most resilient desert animals in the world, has died in the sand. But John has survived. He has skinned that camel and fashioned its hide into a garment to protect him from the stings of bees so that he can eat honey from the comb. He is tough – tougher than anyone you and I ever met by far and away.

Not just physically tough, but mentally tough. In the desert there is no wood for campfires. I'm a survival teacher, as many of you know, and I can tell you firsthand that the first time you spend a night alone in the middle of nowhere without a campfire, the darkness of the nighttime world collapses in on you. Every sound makes you jump. You cannot relax. If you are in the woods, all you can do is obsess about an approaching bear you cannot see, or think about the silent, deadly ticks you cannot feel or see that are drinking your blood. When you are in the desert, all you do is think about are the snakes and scorpions that are crawling up around you to steal your warmth.

But, once you acclimate and overcome your fears, you get to see and experience things others have not. You get to watch the moon rising slow and clear, illuminating the world around you. Sitting still in a moonlit clearing without a fire, I have had fox walk right up to me, nose to nose, and give me a curious sniff. In the desert, at night, far away from the lights of the city, you get a view of the sky you can get nowhere else. The first night I spent in the desert, I lay on my back and looked upward. The depth of the perspective was so breathtaking that it triggered my fear of heights. I felt as though I was going to fall upward into a limitless heaven filled with stars.

So I ask you – who is John the Baptist? He's tough, resilient, careful, precise, wise, and completely unafraid. He makes puny, pampered people like you and me – and the city folks who come out into the desert to be baptized! – look like mere babes in diapers. When John the Baptist tells you that you need to take a hard look at yourself and get yourself straightened out, that you need to confess your sins and be baptized, you respectfully shut your mouth and take heed.

And guess what? Jesus, just as John did, went into the desert. For forty days and forty nights, he confronted his human fears, fought the devil, and returned home alive. And as soon as he returns from his temptation, what does Jesus do? He proclaims, "The time is fulfilled and the Kingdom of God is at hand: repent and believe in the gospel" (Mark 1:15).

This is one of the reasons why we read that Jesus "taught them as one that had authority, and not as the scribes" (Mark 1:22). When someone who has braved forty days alone in the desert speaks, people listen. Jesus and John the Baptist braved dangers few of us will ever face, saw sights few of us will ever see, and died to the comforts of the world so they could live unto God. This is one of the many reasons why people of their day listened to them, and why we would do well to listen to them now.

Third Sunday of Advent, Dec. 11ᵗʰ, 2022

Readings: Is 35:1-6a, 10, Ps 146:6-7, 8-9, 9-10, Jas 5:7-10, Mt 11:2-11

<u>Matthew 11:2-11 World English Bible Catholic Edition</u>

2 Now when John heard in the prison the works of Christ, he sent two of his disciples 3 and said to him, "Are you he who comes, or should we look for another?"

4 Jesus answered them, "Go and tell John the things which you hear and see: 5 the blind receive their sight, the lame walk, the lepers are cleansed, the deaf hear, ✡ the dead are raised up, and the poor have good news preached to them. ✡ 6 Blessed is he who finds no occasion for stumbling in me."

7 As these went their way, Jesus began to say to the multitudes concerning John, "What did you go out into the wilderness to see? A reed shaken by the wind? 8 But what did you go out to see? A man in soft clothing? Behold, those who wear soft clothing are in kings' houses. 9 But why did you go out? To see a prophet? Yes, I tell you, and much more than a prophet. 10 For this is he, of whom it is written, 'Behold, I send my messenger before your face, who will prepare your way before you.' ✡ 11 Most certainly I tell you, among those who are born of women there has not arisen anyone greater than John the Baptizer; yet he who is least in the Kingdom of Heaven is greater than he.

The blind, deaf, and mute are everywhere. You may be one of them, or so may I, from time to time or from moment to moment. Blind to the suffering of others. Unable to see a way through the fog of life, deaf to the cries of those who are suffering, unable to make out the pleas for help coming from our loved ones, or from the depths of our own souls for that matter. Unable to speak our minds, incapable of properly expressing our thoughts. Literally or figuratively, we have all been, or are now, blind, deaf, and mute.

Maybe you can't see past your bills or your health issues. Maybe you can't see a future beyond your addiction, your physical disability, or your grief. Remember though, Jesus sympathizes. He has been there. How hard was it for him to see past the blood in his eyes that ran down from the crown of thorns on his brow? Pray to him. Ask him, "Lord, how did you bear this kind of misery? Show me the way. Shine a light on my dark path." He will be there.

Maybe you can't hear the Word of God over the racket of cell phones, TikTok, social media, pop culture, and fashion. Maybe you're tone deaf and you don't even realize it. Pray to Lord. Say, "What are my spouse and children calling out for? Love? Attention? Engagement? What's my boss or mentor asking of me that I'm not paying attention to? What am I ignoring? Lord, what is your plan for my life?" The Lord will answer. He's been there. How hard was it to hear over the pounding of the nails into his hands and feet on the cross? And when he answers you, listen. Take action. You might even have a happier family, build stronger friendships, get a raise, or find your true calling!

It's also easy to be mute in this world – hard to bend your knee in prayer sometimes, Hard to be a proper witness of the Gospel, hard to find the right words when topics are awkward. Perhaps you need to have a serious talk with a loved one but, but you've been holding your tongue out of fear that one of you will get angry. Do you need to have a talk with your boss, or a difficult employee? Is there a confession you need to make to your guidance counselor, therapist, priest, or to the police? Ask the Lord to be your intermediary. Pray for him to take your hand and fill your mouth with perfect, polite, patient, and measured words.

Remember, the Lord has been there too, standing before Pilate in the crosshairs, under threat of death. He knows. He understands. He will help. And with his help, you will find your voice. You may even sing.

Fourth Sunday of Advent, Dec. 18th, 2022

Readings: Is 7:10-14, Ps 24:1-2, 3-4, 5-6, Rom 1:1-7, Mt 1:18-24

<u>Psalm 24</u>

1 The earth is the LORD's, with its fullness;
the world, and those who dwell in it.
2 For he has founded it on the seas,
and established it on the floods.
3 Who may ascend to the LORD's hill?
Who may stand in his holy place?
4 He who has clean hands and a pure heart;
who has not lifted up his soul to falsehood,
and has not sworn deceitfully.
5 He shall receive a blessing from the LORD,
righteousness from the God of his salvation.
6 This is the generation of those who seek Him,
who seek your face—even Jacob.
Selah.
7 Lift up your heads, you gates!
Be lifted up, you everlasting doors,
and the King of glory will come in.
8 Who is the King of glory?
The LORD strong and mighty,
the LORD mighty in battle.
9 Lift up your heads, you gates;

yes, lift them up, you everlasting doors,
and the King of glory will come in.
10 Who is this King of glory?
The LORD of Armies is the King of glory!
<u>Matthew 1:18-24 World English Bible</u>

18 Now the birth of Jesus Christ was like this: After his mother, Mary, was engaged to Joseph, before they came together, she was found pregnant by the Holy Spirit. 19 Joseph, her husband, being a righteous man, and not willing to make her a public example, intended to put her away secretly. 20 But when he thought about these things, behold,§ an angel of the Lord appeared to him in a dream, saying, "Joseph, son of David, don't be afraid to take to yourself Mary as your wife, for that which is conceived in her is of the Holy Spirit. 21 She shall give birth to a son. You shall name him Jesus, for it is he who shall save his people from their sins."*

22 Now all this has happened that it might be fulfilled which was spoken by the Lord through the prophet, saying,

23 "Behold, the virgin shall be with child,

and shall give birth to a son.

They shall call his name Immanuel,"

which is, being interpreted, "God with us."✡

24 Joseph arose from his sleep, and did as the angel of the Lord commanded him, and took his wife to himself; 25 and didn't know her sexually until she had given birth to her firstborn son. He named him Jesus.

How does our Lord enter into his creation? After all, God is not a being in the world, not some kind of sky fairy, not a being living somewhere in the universe. He's not a super powerful alien vacationing in Maui or hiding in a distant galaxy. As the uncaused cause of existence itself, we cannot find him in the material world. We cannot open a book, rifle the pages, and expect the author to fall out like a pressed flower.

So I ask again: how does God enter into his creation? Does he smash his way in like an intruder? Does he enter by war, patricide, and retribution the way that the Greco-Roman gods did? Is he born of a giant, like Odin?

No. Our Lord enters by faith. Mary is visited by the archangel Gabriel and told her destiny is to be the Mother of God. Does she say, "Please, no! My husband and his family will never believe this really happened, and he'll divorce me!" No, she says instead, "Let it be done to me according to your word." (Luke 1:38). What does Joseph do and say when the archangel Gabriel appears to him? Does he reject the news? Does he allow pride and doubt interfere with his belief? No. He believes. He has faith in his bride's fidelity, faith in the angel, and most importantly, faith in God!

And when does the Lord enter his creation? Does he show up, like the old pagan gods did, at some point in the misty, shady, prehistoric past? No indeed! It's no coincidence that the world clock reset to zero at the birth of Jesus, and that we number the years according to his birth. Jesus is born during history. There are no eyewitness accounts to the myths of the old gods. Jesus' mother and father are alive into his adulthood, even into his ministry. At the time his story is recorded, there are living observers to the events in his childhood. The Lord enters his creation, not just mythically, but literally. In the here and now.

How appropriate it is that we should find Psalm 24 paired with this passage from the Gospel of St. Matthew. Because Psalm 24, my favorite, describes exactly that is going on in the arrival of the infant Jesus.

Faith is the door, the gateway, through which the Lord enters his creation. He does not make a mere symbolic, philosophical entry– it is symbolic and philosophical for sure! – but he also enters as a literal fact in time, in and through the actual choices of two humble people named Mary and Joseph. Our hearts and minds reel with the thought of it! It's so spectacular, so shocking, so extraordinary! Through the gate of their true love and true faith, the Lord enters his creation to save us all.

§1:20 "Behold", from "ἰδού", means look at, take notice, observe, see, or gaze at. It is often used as an interjection.
* *1:21 "Jesus" means "Salvation".*
* ✡1:23 Isaiah 7:14*

The Nativity of the Lord (Christmas), Dec. 25th, 2022

Readings: Is 52:7-10, Ps 98:1, 2-3, 3-4, 5-6., Heb 1:1-6, John 1:1-5, 9-14

<u>John 1:1-5, 9-14 World English Bible</u>

1 In the beginning was the Word, and the Word was with God, and the Word was God. 2 The same was in the beginning with God. 3 All things were made through him. Without him, nothing was made that has been made. 4 In him was life, and the life was the light of men. 5 The light shines in the darkness, and the darkness hasn't overcome it.*

9 The true light that enlightens everyone was coming into the world.

10 He was in the world, and the world was made through him, and the world didn't recognize him. 11 He came to his own, and those who were his own didn't receive him. 12 But as many as received him, to them he gave the right to become God's children, to those who believe in his name: 13 who were born, not of blood, nor of the will of the flesh, nor of the will of man, but of God.

14 The Word became flesh and lived among us. We saw his glory, such glory as of the only born† Son of the Father, full of grace and truth.

Today we celebrate the day angels appeared to shepherds in the hill country and said,

> *Fear not: for, behold, I bring you good tidings of great joy, which shall be to all people. For unto you is born this day in the city of David a Saviour, which is Christ the Lord. (Luke 2:10-11 KJV)*

And today, like those shepherds – metaphorically at least! – we move toward the spiritual City of David where this child is to be found, lying in a feeding trough for animals. Here we partake of the spiritual food which is Christ the Lord. We are those shepherds. And just like the shepherds did after they found the Holy Family as the angel promised, we proclaim the good news far and wide, to friends, our neighbors, and our families.

> *And they came with haste, and found Mary, and Joseph, and the babe lying in a manger. And when they had seen it, they made known abroad the saying which was told them concerning this child. And all they that heard it wondered at those things which were told them by the shepherds. (Luke 1: 16-18 KJV)*

As shepherds, as witnesses of the transforming power of the miracle of the Incarnation, we have good tidings of great joy to share. And this news is desperately needed. Poll after poll, survey after survey, shows that most people outside our faith have one of two views of Christianity. They see it as either a system of mostly political rules and morals they don't agree with, or as just another club or activity selling them spiritual fulfillment as a product.

It's up to us to let them know that Christianity is not a political party or a product. We are not competing with their backpacking club. This is not an organic gardening or Yoga class. For people who feel like they do, Christmas may seem like just another drain on their attention, just another excuse for someone to sell them something, just another chore, just another grab for their pocketbook.

It's up to us to proclaim through our words and actions that Christmas is a holiday like no other, because Jesus is a figure like no other. He is not merely a wise, mortal teacher like Buddha or Plato who lived a long time ago and who encouraged morality, ethics and good manners. No, no – he is the Son of God, true light from true light, true God from true God. He came, not to show us how to be kind and nice, like a really, really, good kindergarten teacher.

He came to show us how to fundamentally remake ourselves in the image of God.

Let everyone know, my fellow shepherds, that Jesus came bringing salvation – liberation from the slavery of selfishness and evil; deliverance from the emptiness and pointlessness of modern life; alleviation of the pain associated with separation from God; and the possibility of never-ending blissful union with him in the life to come.

Let the world know that the Son of God entered his creation so that we might partake of his divine nature. So that, by entering into communion with the Son of God, we might ourselves become sons of God in turn. As St. Athanasius said, "For the Son of God became man so that we might become God."

Merry Christmas to all! And to my fellow shepherds, let us go forth and proclaim the good news!

*1:5 The word translated "overcome" (κατέλαβεν) can also be translated "comprehended." It refers to getting a grip on an enemy to defeat him.

†1:14 The phrase "only born" is from the Greek word "μονογενους", which is sometimes translated "only begotten" or "one and only".

The Circumcision and Naming of Christ, Jan. 1ˢᵗ, 2023

Readings: Num 6:22-end, Ps 8, Gal 4:4-7, Lk 2:15-21

<u>Luke 2:15-21 World English Bible Catholic Edition</u>

When the angels went away from them into the sky, the shepherds said to one another, "Let's go to Bethlehem, now, and see this thing that has happened, which the Lord has made known to us." 16 They came with haste and found both Mary and Joseph, and the baby was lying in the feeding trough. 17 When they saw it, they publicized widely the saying which was spoken to them about this child. 18 All who heard it wondered at the things which were spoken to them by the shepherds. 19 But Mary kept all these sayings, pondering them in her heart. 20 The shepherds returned, glorifying and praising God for all the things that they had heard and seen, just as it was told them.

21 When eight days were fulfilled for the circumcision of the child, his name was called Jesus, which was given by the angel before he was conceived in the womb.

God, the ground of all being, the source and establisher of creation, has no literal gender. Isn't it strange then, that he refers to himself as Father (Ex 4:22-23 for example) and we call him Father? And that he decides to enter into his creation as a male? Why does God approach us as a male rather than female? And why has the circumcision of infant Jesus been deemed important enough to warrant a feast day?

We cannot know the mind of God, but we can suspect that God came as a man for a very pragmatic and practical reason: positive, healthy father figures are central to strong communities and societies. Boys are particularly vulnerable. Ninety percent of all crime is committed by males, and almost ninety percent of them are fatherless. How many men and boys have chosen to be better fathers and better sons by emulating the divine scheme? But this issue cuts across sexes. More than 4 out of 5 youths in prison come from fatherless homes, and fatherless children are six times more likely to life in poverty and to commit criminal acts. It's impossible to know how many fatherless girls and boys have taken comfort in knowing they had a father in heaven, or how much pain and suffering has been alleviated by God's simple choice to present himself as a Father to the world.

Like all Hebrew boys, the Son of God came to be circumcised and named. And for a human male to have the foreskin of his penis cut off is a huge and humbling step, literally and symbolically. In this ritual, ego and masculinity are literally trimmed down to size. But this too cuts across the sexes. Deuteronomy 30:6 reads, "The LORD, your God, will circumcise your hearts and the hearts of your descendants, so that you will love the LORD, your God, with your whole heart and your whole being, in order that you may live." And we read in Jeremiah 4:3-4, "For to the people of Judah and Jerusalem, thus says the LORD: Till your untilled ground, and do not sow among thorns. Be circumcised for the LORD, remove the foreskins of your hearts, people of Judah and inhabitants of Jerusalem; Or else my anger will break out like fire, and burn so that no one can quench it, because of your evil deeds."

This is why St. Paul says in Romans 2:28-29 "For he is not a Jew who is one outwardly, neither is that circumcision which is outward in the flesh; but he is a Jew who is one inwardly, and circumcision is that of the heart, in the spirit, not in the letter; whose praise is not from men, but from God."

The Son of God, our Lord Jesus Christ, sets an eternal example of the circumcision of the heart, humbling himself to enter into our humanity.

In Genesis, God begins creation on the first day of existence itself by declaring "let there be light." He completes his creation in six days, and on the seventh he rests. God's only Son, the Light of the World, is born on Christmas, the dawning of the first day of a new creation. On the eighth day, his Son accepts his circumcision. This is the historical event dated 1/1/1 – the first day, of the first month, in the first year – the event that resets the clock of all humanity and begins our every new year with hearts circumcised in Christ.

The Epiphany of the Lord, 1/8/23

Readings: Is 60:1-6, Ps 72:1-2, 7-8, 10-11, 12-13., Eph 3:2-3a, 5-6, Mt 2:1-12

<u>Matthew 2:1-12 World English Bible Catholic Edition</u>

1 Now when Jesus was born in Bethlehem of Judea in the days of King Herod, behold, wise men from the east came to Jerusalem, saying, 2 "Where is he who is born King of the Jews? For we saw his star in the east, and have come to worship him." 3 When King Herod heard it, he was troubled, and all Jerusalem with him. 4 Gathering together all the chief priests and scribes of the people, he asked them where the Christ would be born. 5 They said to him, "In Bethlehem of Judea, for this is written through the prophet,*

6 'You Bethlehem, land of Judah,

are in no way least among the princes of Judah;

for out of you shall come a governor

who shall shepherd my people, Israel.' "✡

7 Then Herod secretly called the wise men, and learned from them exactly what time the star appeared. 8 He sent them to Bethlehem, and said, "Go and search diligently for the young child. When you have found him, bring me word, so that I also may come and worship him."

9 They, having heard the king, went their way; and behold, the star, which they saw in the east, went before them until it came and stood over where the young child was. 10 When they saw the star, they rejoiced with exceedingly great joy.

11 They came into the house and saw the young child with Mary, his mother, and they fell down and worshiped him. Opening their treasures, they offered to him gifts: gold, frankincense, and myrrh. 12 Being warned in a dream not to return to Herod, they went back to their own country another way.

In the ancient world, there was no grand plan. For the Greeks, the Romans, the shamans of Asia, the Slavic pagans, the druids, the Celts and the Vikings – all of the world's ancient cultures – there was no time as we know it today. They looked up into the heavens, and they saw repeating patterns of stars. They saw recurring seasons. Every year was just like the last. They assumed that every year in the past had been like the present one, and every year in the future would be the same.

Each individual historian kept time independently. This one marked the time since the reign of a certain monarch, another by the number of seasons since this or that war, or the number of years since the foundation of a given empire. It wasn't until Christianity burst onto the scene this all changed. The years began to be marked as before Christ or after Christ – BC and AD.

But even after Judeo-Christian culture began to mark universal time, scientists – and this is not a coincidence! – scientists picked up the pagan banner of steady-state time. Scientists and pagan unbelievers were united in their disbelief. Cosmologists – these are the astronomers who study the origin of the universe and the formation of its galaxies, solar systems, suns, planets, and moons – were just like the pagans of the ancient world. Cosmologists thought that the universe had always been, and it would always be, the same. That is, until a physicist and cosmologist by the name of Fr. Georges Lemaître – a Roman Catholic priest – rocked the scientific establishment. Lemaître's "Big Bang Theory" is now taught in every school in the world.

What this means is that the universe came to be at a particular point in time. And at a particular point in time, it will cease to be. Judeo-Christians knew this all along of course. We know that God is the source and establisher of creation. We read in Gen 1:14, *Then God said, "Let there be lights in the expanse of the heavens to separate the day from the night, and they shall serve as signs and for seasons, and for days and years."*

We know that God created the universe and put into place the stars and planets and established the very laws of physics that scientists use to prove and disprove their theories.

We know that the greatest scientists and astronomers of Jesus' day – pagans from Babylon known as the magi – used their scientific methods to determine that something incredible had happened: the King of the Jews and the Savior of the world had been born.

We knew then, and we know now, what everyone in the world must surely know just by looking at the date: that time begins and ends with God, and human time is measured by the birth of Jesus Christ.

Let us pray, brothers and sisters, that the world's pagans, skeptics, and idolators of materialism, come to embrace the greater truth of Christ embedded in the science which they hold true. Let us pray they each have their individual epiphanies: that they journey westward bearing their gifts, and kneel before the King of the Universe who is Christ the Lord.

* 2:1 The word for "wise men" (magoi) can also mean teachers, scientists, physicians, astrologers, seers, interpreters of dreams, or sorcerers.

✡ 2:6 Micah 5:2

2nd Sunday in Ordinary Time, 1/15/23

Readings: Is 49:3, 5-6, Ps 40:2, 4, 7-8, 8-9, 10, 1 Cor 1:1-3, Jn 1:29-34

<u>John 1:29-34 World English Bible Catholic Edition</u>

29 The next day, he saw Jesus coming to him, and said, "Behold,† the Lamb of God, who takes away the sin of the world! 30 This is he of whom I said, 'After me comes a man who is preferred before me, for he was before me.' 31 I didn't know him, but for this reason I came baptizing in water, that he would be revealed to Israel." 32 John testified, saying, "I have seen the Spirit descending like a dove out of heaven, and it remained on him. 33 I didn't recognize him, but he who sent me to baptize in water said to me, 'On whomever you will see the Spirit descending and remaining on him is he who baptizes in the Holy Spirit.' 34 I have seen and have testified that this is the Son of God."

Today's epistle reading from 1 Corinthians is a little hard to understand, depending on the translation. Paul says,

Paul, called to be an apostle of Jesus Christ through the will of God, and our brother Sosthenes, 2 to the assembly of God which is at Corinth—those who are sanctified in Christ Jesus, called saints, with all who call on the name of our Lord Jesus*

Christ in every place, both theirs and ours: 3 Grace to you and peace from God our Father and the Lord Jesus Christ.

And once you figure it out, it seems so mundane. You think, "Oh, I get it. But it's just the salutation of a letter – what are we supposed to learn from this?" Well, rest assured, like most everything Saint Paul says, his simple greeting to fellow Christians in Corinth is jam-packed with meaning.

Paul makes it clear that the message he is sending isn't coming from him alone, but also from his brother in Christ, Sosthenes. And, furthermore, he emphasizes that he and Sosthenes are joined together in holiness with those he's addressing who are in Corinth, as well as with everyone who calls on the name of Christ. The very next thing Paul says to them is,

"Now I beg you, brothers and sisters, through the name of our Lord, Jesus Christ, that you all speak the same thing, and that there be no divisions among you, but that you be perfected together in the same mind and in the same judgment."

Let this be a warning to us also my friends. We must always and everywhere be witnesses of Christ in our thoughts, desires, actions, and beliefs – in our words and in our hearts – or else our message will not get through clearly. And you may ask, "What's the message?"

We are the message.

Our words? Yes. But also our demeanor, our choices, our attitude, our body language—all of it. If a picture is worth a thousand words, how many words is a cold shoulder worth? How many volumes does a betrayal speak? One callous comment is a trumpet blast, each insensitivity is a volcanic eruption.

In my evangelism work, I can't tell you how often I hear comments like,

- "I left my church because the people there were jerks."
- "Christians are all judgmental prudes and nitwits."
- "Christians think they're perfect and everybody else is going to hell."
- "Priests and pastors are just leeches on society."

These statements are far from true. But it's a fact that every misbegotten word, inappropriate comment, and cutting glance falls like a domino, and leads we know not where. We are wise if we remember the words of James 1:26,

> *"If anyone among you thinks himself to be religious while he doesn't bridle his tongue, but deceives his heart, this man's religion is worthless."*

† 1:14 The phrase "only born" is from the Greek word "μονογενους", which is sometimes translated "only begotten" or "one and only."

*1:1 "Christ" means "Anointed One."

3rd Sunday in Ordinary Time, 1/22/23

Readings: Is 8:23—9:3, Ps 27:1, 4, 13-14, 1 Cor 1:10-13, 17, Mt 4:12-23

<u>Matthew 4:12-23 World English Bible Catholic Edition</u>

12 Now when Jesus heard that John was delivered up, he withdrew into Galilee. 13 Leaving Nazareth, he came and lived in Capernaum, which is by the sea, in the region of Zebulun and Naphtali, 14 that it might be fulfilled which was spoken through Isaiah the prophet, saying,

15 "The land of Zebulun and the land of Naphtali,

toward the sea, beyond the Jordan,

Galilee of the Gentiles,

16 the people who sat in darkness saw a great light;

to those who sat in the region and shadow of death,

to them light has dawned."✡

17 From that time, Jesus began to preach, and to say, "Repent! For the Kingdom of Heaven is at hand."

18 Walking by the sea of Galilee, he† saw two brothers: Simon, who is called Peter, and Andrew, his brother, casting a net into the sea; for they were fishermen. 19 He said to them, "Come after me, and I will make you fishers for men."

20 They immediately left their nets and followed him. 21 Going on from there, he saw two other brothers, James the son of Zebedee, and John his brother, in the boat with Zebedee their father, mending their nets. He called them. 22 They immediately left the boat and their father, and followed him.

23 Jesus went about in all Galilee, teaching in their synagogues, preaching the Good News of the Kingdom, and healing every disease and every sickness among the people. 24 The report about him went out into all Syria. They brought to him all who were sick, afflicted with various diseases and torments, possessed with demons, epileptics, and paralytics; and he healed them. 25 Great multitudes from Galilee, Decapolis, Jerusalem, Judea, and from beyond the Jordan followed him.

You know, I have four kids, all grown up now and living on their own. But when things go wrong, when they are deeply saddened, they come home. Sometimes for a day, sometimes for a week. They need that security. They need to regroup. And that's what Jesus did. When St. John the Baptist is arrested and thrown into the Black Fortress of Machaerus, Jesus goes home to Nazareth.

But you know, after they regroup – after they eat some home cooking and get some fatherly and motherly advice from my wife and I – my kids realize they have to go back to their lives, back to their jobs, back out into the crazy world and continue their adventures. And so, Jesus leaves home and goes to Capernaum, a bustling city of the gentiles sitting right on a major trade route, modern and eclectic, on the edge of the Sea of Galilee. And there he starts his mission in earnest, finding his first apostles.

Did this literally happen? I believe it did. But I also believe that this is a metaphorical story. As St. Paul says in today's epistle reading, we must be careful about getting so wrapped up "human eloquence" – that is, human literal interpretations and the people who offer them to us – that we lose sight of the Cross and empty the Gospel of its fullest meaning.

So, may I suggest that this section of Matthew is a philosophical lesson as well. It's about how we think, and solve, and fix problems. When we get shocking, unexpected news – like Jesus finding out that his beloved cousin has been thrown in prison – it shatters our worldview. We don't know quite what to think or do. So we retreat to the familiar – we go home to familiar places, familiar ideas, and familiar solutions. But in the end, in order to solve a new problem, we need new information and a fresh perspective. We can't stay home. Literally, like going to Capernaum of the gentiles, or to a new intellectual place, like a reading a new book, talking to new people, considering new perspectives.

We have to swim in a different sea of ideas. The Gospels repeatedly refer to the lake adjacent to Capernaum as the "Sea of Galilee." But it's not a sea. It's a big lake. It's fresh water. The gospel writers weren't stupid, they knew what it was. They called a "sea" on purpose. Because "sea" is a bigger word, a richer word. We cannot see into the depths of the sea. There can be good and bad in the depths – there can be a great catch, or a sea monster. The weather changes rapidly on the sea. We might have a pleasant day of sailing, or we might be shipwrecked. We could have a pleasant swim, or we could drown.

And so, along the edge of the sea – walking on the edge where the safe and familiar make contact with the dangerous and mysterious – Jesus finds and calls his first apostles. Jesus himself is on the cutting edge, breathing new and fresh ways of seeing and thinking into the old ways of the Hebrews. And from there he goes on to do the miraculous work of heal the sick and casting out demons.

Like Jesus, we can't stay home when things go wrong. We must have the courage to go to new places and cast our nets into the seas of discovery and innovation for fresh perspectives. And, if we carefully integrate what we draw up with our familiar, time-tested wisdom, we too have the hope of solving great problems and making new and very important friends.

4th Sunday in Ordinary Time, 1/29/23

Readings: Zep 2:3; 3:12-13, Ps 146:6-7, 8-9, 9-10, 1 Cor 1:26-31, Mt 5:1-12a

<u>Matthew 5:1-12a World English Bible Catholic Edition</u>

1 Seeing the multitudes, he went up onto the mountain. When he had sat down, his disciples came to him. 2 He opened his mouth and taught them, saying,

3 "Blessed are the poor in spirit,

for theirs is the Kingdom of Heaven. ✡

4 Blessed are those who mourn,

for they shall be comforted. ✡

5 Blessed are the gentle,

for they shall inherit the earth. *✡

6 Blessed are those who hunger and thirst for righteousness,

for they shall be filled.

7 Blessed are the merciful,

for they shall obtain mercy.

8 Blessed are the pure in heart,

for they shall see God.

9 Blessed are the peacemakers,

for they shall be called children of God.

10 Blessed are those who have been persecuted for righteousness' sake,

for theirs is the Kingdom of Heaven.

11 "Blessed are you when people reproach you, persecute you, and say all kinds of evil against you falsely, for my sake. 12 Rejoice, and be exceedingly glad, for great is your reward in heaven.

These are the opening lines of the most incredible speech ever delivered by a spiritual teacher in all of history – the speech that establishes the foundation of Christianity itself. These influential words have shaped and inspired billions of people down the two millennia since they were spoken, both Christians and non-Christians, like religious pluralist liberator Mahatma Gandhi and agnostic author of <u>Brave New World</u> Aldous Huxley.

To deliver these words, Jesus chooses a mountain, yet he sits eye-to-eye. Fully God and fully man, he speaks at once as God, from a high place, but as a man, on our level. The scripture says, "he opened his mouth and taught them." The Bible is sparse, not rambling. Every word matters. So what's important about him opening his mouth? Doesn't everyone open their mouth to speak? Are we expecting Jesus to be a ventriloquist? No, he opened his mouth to speak. He didn't just repeat the words of other prophets. He spoke as one who has authority, not like a scribe reading the words of the ancient prophets (Mt 7:29).

And what does he say? Using a similar verbal format, but changing the message, Jesus turns the message of the previous prophets inside out. He subverts the old rhetoric. We know what the old messages sound like, especially from Proverbs and Psalms.

- "Honor the Lord with your substance and with the first fruits of all our produce, then your barns will be filled with plenty and your vats will be overflowing with new wine." (Proverbs 3:9-10).
- "Blessed is the man who doesn't walk in the counsel of the wicked, nor stand on the path of sinners" (Psalm 1:1).
- "Blessed is he whose disobedience is forgiven, whose sin is covered. Blessed is the man to whom Yahweh doesn't impute iniquity, in whose spirit there is no deceit." (Psalm 32:1-2).

Jesus offers a new perspective. Yes, sometimes things go well when we think and act in accord with God's commandments. Yes, sometimes God answers our prayers. But when things don't go the way we want, despite our prayers and despite playing by the rules to the best of our ability, Jesus wants us to take heart and know that we are still blessed.

God is not a far-off God, an uncaring and legalistic God, or a merely a God of covenants. He is a God who sympathizes with our feelings of sadness and mourning, with our feelings of injustice and unfairness. This is why he comes down to earth as Immanuel, which means "God is with us" (Isaiah 7:14, Mt 1:29).

On a high mountain he sits down with us, looks us in the eye, and opens his mouth.

✡ 5:3 Isaiah 57:15; 66:2

✡5:4 Isaiah 61:2; 66:10,13
*5:5 or, land.
✡5:5 Psalm 37:11

5th Sunday in Ordinary Time, 2/5/23

Readings: Is 58:7-10, Ps 112:4-5, 6-7, 8-9, 1 Cor 2:1-5, Mt 5:13-16

<u>Matthew 5:13-16 World English Bible Catholic Edition</u>

13 "You are the salt of the earth, but if the salt has lost its flavor, with what will it be salted? It is then good for nothing, but to be cast out and trodden under the feet of men.

14 You are the light of the world. A city located on a hill can't be hidden. 15 Neither do you light a lamp and put it under a measuring basket, but on a stand; and it shines to all who are in the house. 16 Even so, let your light shine before men, that they may see your good works and glorify your Father who is in heaven.

Our relationship with salt and light is much different today than it was two millennia ago. We take salt and light for granted. These days, we are told to watch our salt intake. The doctor wants us to keep it below 2,300 mg a day, but the average American takes in around 3,400, almost 50% more than recommended. We get too much salt!

But in Jesus' time, salt was a precious commodity, sometimes used as international currency. Every major city in the ancient world was built near a liberal salt source. Solnitsata in Bulgaria is the oldest town in Europe, and it was built around a salt mine. Salt was the only reliable means of preserving food in those days. Every army ran on salt rations, which is the origin of the phrase, "earning your salt." The word *salary* comes from the Latin *salarium* which means "related to salt." There was little processed food in those days, and getting enough salt was far more difficult – especially when you consider that a typical, pre-industrial manual laborer burns up to three-and-a-half times as many calories as we modern folks do! Lack of salt causes headaches, weakness, muscle aches and cramps, and in extreme cases, death.

What about light? Light pollution is one of reasons that modern people don't get enough rest. Street lights, headlights, flashlights, flood lights and garden footlights make the outdoor environment awash with light. Cellphones, tablets, and TV screens do the same indoors. Almost every appliance has some kind of glowing clock, display, or LED light on it. The power lights on my cable box and digital router are so bright I can practically read by them.

But light was an expensive resource in Jesus' day. The average person used the cheapest fats and oils to power lamps, which meant that for common people, lamps were smelly, smoky, and hard to keep going. Only the wealthy could afford to burn the good stuff, and could enjoy clear, odor-free, consistent illumination. And gathering and cutting wood was hard work. Who would want to waste it on bonfires?

Okay. So now, as modern disciples, let's hear Jesus' words with the same ears with which the disciples heard them all those years ago. We are the salt of the earth. We bring the words, the teaching, the messages that make the world function. We are the salt that keeps laborers producing good works. We ensure that the shepherds of men will not tire of leading their flocks, that soldiers fighting in the war against evil will not falter, and that political and social bodies will not seize up, cramp, and stumble. We are the salt that preserves God's wisdom and allows it to be feed the world's hungry millions!

Jesus wants us to be the essential element of the culture, to be the substance that energizes its essential functions. He wants us to illuminate the society from within, the way a lamp brightens a home and the way a city's bonfires make it visible from afar. To all of those wayfarers wandering in the darkness of confusion and ignorance, depression and anxiety, hopelessness and nihilism, he wants us to be a beacon.

6th Sunday in Ordinary Time, 2/12/23

Readings: Sir 15:15-20, Ps 119:1-2, 4-5, 17-18, 33-34, 1 Cor 2:6-10, Mt 5:17-37

<u>Matthew 5:17-37 World English Bible Catholic Edition</u>

17 *"Don't think that I came to destroy the law or the prophets. I didn't come to destroy, but to fulfill. 18 For most certainly, I tell you, until heaven and earth pass away, not even one smallest letter† or one tiny pen stroke‡ shall in any way pass away from the law, until all things are accomplished. 19 Therefore, whoever shall break one of these least commandments and teach others to do so, shall be called least in the Kingdom of Heaven; but whoever shall do and teach them shall be called great in the Kingdom of Heaven. 20 For I tell you that unless your righteousness exceeds that of the scribes and Pharisees, there is no way you will enter into the Kingdom of Heaven.*

21 *"You have heard that it was said to the ancient ones, 'You shall not murder;'✡ and 'Whoever murders will be in danger of the judgment.' 22 But I tell you that everyone who is angry with his brother without a cause § will be in danger of the judgment. Whoever says to his brother, 'Raca!' * will be in danger of the council. Whoever says, 'You fool!' will be in danger of the fire of Gehenna.†*

23 *"If therefore you are offering your gift at the altar, and there remember that your brother has anything against you, 24 leave your gift there before the altar, and go your way. First be reconciled to your brother, and then come and offer your gift. 25 Agree with your adversary quickly while you are with him on the way; lest perhaps the prosecutor deliver you to the judge, and the judge deliver you to the officer, and you be cast into prison. 26 Most certainly I tell you, you shall by no means get out of there until you have paid the last penny.*‡

27 *"You have heard that it was said,* § *'You shall not commit adultery;'*✡ *28 but I tell you that everyone who gazes at a woman to lust after her has committed adultery with her already in his heart. 29 If your right eye causes you to stumble, pluck it out and throw it away from you. For it is more profitable for you that one of your members should perish than for your whole body to be cast into Gehenna.* * *30 If your right hand causes you to stumble, cut it off, and throw it away from you. For it is more profitable for you that one of your members should perish, than for your whole body to be cast into Gehenna.*†

31 *"It was also said, 'Whoever shall put away his wife, let him give her a writing of divorce,'*✡ *32 but I tell you that whoever puts away his wife, except for the cause of sexual immorality, makes her an adulteress; and whoever marries her when she is put away commits adultery.*

33 *"Again you have heard that it was said to the ancient ones, 'You shall not make false vows, but shall perform to the Lord your vows,'*✡ *34 but I tell you, don't swear at all: neither by heaven, for it is the throne of God; 35 nor by the earth, for it is the footstool of his feet; nor by Jerusalem, for it is the city of the*

great King. 36 Neither shall you swear by your head, for you can't make one hair white or black. 37 But let your 'Yes' be 'Yes' and your 'No' be 'No.' Whatever is more than these is of the evil one.

The expression "the spirit of the law" is widely used by Christians and non-Christians alike, and I believe today's gospel reading is its origin. We are all well aware of the problem. We know that we must have laws and rules. Without them we'd be crippled by the chaos of contention, confusion, and conflict. But for every set of rules there will always be people who specialize in exploiting the gaps between the rules in order take advantage, rather than attempting to sincerely adhere to them.

We all know what this looks like. In sports, when one team is ahead, it's perfectly legal to run out the clock. But it's not in the true spirit of competition to win a basketball game by dribbling, passing, and playing keep-away; nor is it in the true spirit of sport for a quarterback to take a knee to prevent the other team from having any opportunity to get a turnover and score a last-second touchdown.

Lawyers are another great example. When they twist, manipulate, and take advantage of the rules, prosecute the innocent, or lie in the defense of the depraved, we are appalled. Their willful disregard for the spirit of the law results in shocking miscarriages of justice – the guilty go free, the innocent are punished, and the only winner is the crooked attorney who banks his fee.

It's good that we appreciate the true intent of laws and rules, and that we push back against perversions and exploitations of them. That's great, as far as it goes. But Jesus tells us in today's reading, that we need to go far, far deeper than that. He wants us to embody the spirit of the law – the Holy Spirit. He wants us to keep God's laws inherently, by naturally embodying the characteristics that conform to the laws. He's looking for fundamental change through the power of the Holy Spirit.

We are far too weak and faulty to do this by sheer force of will. If we're to have any hope of being absent of anger, we need the Holy Spirit. If we're going rid ourselves of the lust of our eyes, we need the Holy Spirit. If we're to be completely faithful in our obligations, we need the Holy Spirit. Let us pray that the Holy Spirit may descend upon us as it descended upon Christ and in turn upon the disciples at Pentecost, and that, to the highest degree possible in keeping with our human nature, we might personify the consciousness of Christ.

‡5:18 or, serif

✡5:21 Exodus 20:13

§5:22 NU omits "without a cause".

*5:22 "Raca" is an Aramaic insult, related to the word for "empty" and conveying the idea of empty-headedness.

†5:22 or, Hell

‡5:26 literally, *kodrantes*. A *kodrantes* was a small copper coin worth about 2 lepta (widow's mites)—not enough to buy very much of anything.

§5:27 TR adds "to the ancients".

✡5:27 Exodus 20:14

*5:29 or, Hell

†5:30 or, Hell

✡5:31 Deuteronomy 24:1

✡5:33 Numbers 30:2; Deuteronomy 23:21; Ecclesiastes 5:4

7th Sunday in Ordinary Time, 2/19/23

Readings: Lv 19:1-2, 17-18, Ps 103:1-2, 3-4, 8, 10, 12-13, 1 Cor 3:16-23, Mt 5:38-48

Mt 5:38-48 World English Bible Catholic Edition

38 "You have heard that it was said, 'An eye for an eye, and a tooth for a tooth.' ✡ 39 But I tell you, don't resist him who is evil; but whoever strikes you on your right cheek, turn to him the other also. 40 If anyone sues you to take away your coat, let him have your cloak also. 41 Whoever compels you to go one mile, go with him two. 42 Give to him who asks you, and don't turn away him who desires to borrow from you.

43 "You have heard that it was said, 'You shall love your neighbor ✡ and hate your enemy.'‡ 44 But I tell you, love your enemies, bless those who curse you, do good to those who hate you, and pray for those who mistreat you and persecute you, 45 that you may be children of your Father who is in heaven. For he makes his sun to rise on the evil and the good, and sends rain on the just and the unjust. 46 For if you love those who love you, what reward do you have? Don't even the tax collectors do the same? 47 If you only greet your friends, what more do you do than others? Don't even the tax collectors§ do the same? 48 Therefore you shall be perfect, just as your Father in heaven is perfect.

Friends, the words "be perfect just as your Father in heaven is perfect" can be daunting, especially to those struggling with their faith the way I remember doing years ago. Back then, these words hit me like a hammer. I thought, "This is impossible. Nobody can be perfect! I quit."

But Jesus isn't saying that we need to be perfect in our *execution*, but rather in our *orientation*. He knows that, despite trying our best to be Christ-like, we're fallen beings in a fallen world who have no hope of attaining perfection until the end of days. Let me suggest that what Jesus is saying is that we need to be perfect in our standpoint with respect to the world.

And so, for a little help with this, let's turn to today's epistle reading from 1 Corinthians. These readings really are an ideal pairing because they so effectively help us understand Jesus' command "to be perfect." St. Paul says,

> *For it is written, "He has taken the wise in their craftiness." ✡ 20 And again, "The Lord knows the reasoning of the wise, that it is worthless." ✡ 21 Therefore let no one boast in men. For all things are yours, 22 whether Paul, or Apollos, or Cephas, or the world, or life, or death, or things present, or things to come. All are yours, 23 and you are Christ's, and Christ is God's.*

All things, St. Paul says, belong to us because we belong to nothing less than God. You might say that, because we are not possessed by ideologies, political parties, and cults of personality, we suppose that our leaders should serve us rather than the reverse. They are our leaders. Because we do not belong to the world – we aren't slaves to our desires for food, sex, fame, money, and power – the world is ours. Because we are not slaves to the negative actions of others – not controlled by vengeful thoughts – our actions are ours. Because our lives belong to Christ, we don't fear death. And finally, this means that our present and future lives belong to us. All this and more is ours because we abide in Christ and he in us (John 15:4).

Let us then adopt a perfect standpoint with respect to the world, and "be perfect, just as our heavenly Father is perfect."

✡ 1 Cor 3:19 Job 5:13

   ✡ 1 Cor 3:20 Psalm 94:11

   ✡Mt 5:38 Exodus 21:24; Leviticus 24:20; Deuteronomy 19:21

   ✡ Mt 5:43 Leviticus 19:18

   ‡ Mt 5:43 not in the Bible, but see Qumran Manual of Discipline Ix, 21-26

   § Mt 5:47 NU reads "Gentiles" instead of "tax collectors".

Ash Wednesday, 2/22/23

Readings: Jl 2:12-18, Ps 51:3-4, 5-6ab, 12-13, 14 and 17, 2 Cor 5:20—6:2, Mt 6:1-6, 16-18

Mt 6:1-6, 16-18 World English Bible Catholic Edition

1 "Be careful that you don't do your charitable giving before men, to be seen by them, or else you have no reward from your Father who is in heaven. 2 Therefore, when you do merciful deeds, don't sound a trumpet before yourself, as the hypocrites do in the synagogues and in the streets, that they may get glory from men. Most certainly I tell you, they have received their reward. 3 But when you do merciful deeds, don't let your left hand know what your right hand does, 4 so that your merciful deeds may be in secret, then your Father who sees in secret will reward you openly.*

5 "When you pray, you shall not be as the hypocrites, for they love to stand and pray in the synagogues and in the corners of the streets, that they may be seen by men. Most certainly, I tell you, they have received their reward. 6 But you, when you pray, enter into your inner room, and having shut your door, pray to your Father who is in secret; and your Father who sees in secret will reward you openly.

16 "Moreover when you fast, don't be like the hypocrites, with sad faces. For they disfigure their faces that they may be seen by men to be fasting. Most certainly I tell you, they have received

*their reward. 17 But you, when you fast, anoint your head and
wash your face, 18 so that you are not seen by men to be fasting,
but by your Father who is in secret; and your Father, who sees
in secret, will reward you.*

Brothers and sisters, the world in which we live is always threatened
by chaos and malevolence, brought on by the forces of the Devil and
by the sin and evil of human hearts and hands. Even now a war is
raging in Ukraine. Here in America, about ten churches per day close
their doors forever as backs are turned on God and eyes look down
to earthly rewards rather than upward toward the supernal. Negativity,
hopelessness, and hedonism are the hallmarks of our culture's
direction.

And yet!

And yet, the ash here on the altar made from the palm fronds
from last year's Palm Sunday service, call to mind the Lord's triumphal
entrance into Jerusalem and his victory over Hell. Jesus began his fight
against evil by entering into the wilderness for forty days, by resisting
temptation, and by defeating the Devil. Let us recommit to our mission
by entering the desert of Lent with humble hearts; by reminding
ourselves of our mortality; by doing battle against evil uprisings from
without and from within.

Take heart all who hear. Wash your face, as the savior said, and
enter into the battle with bright faces and anointed heads!

* 6:1 NU reads "acts of righteousness" instead of "charitable giving"

1st Sunday of Lent, Sunday 2/26/23

Readings: Gn 2:7-9; 3:1-7, Ps 51:3-4, 5-6, 12-13, 14 and 17, Rom 5:12-19, Mt 4:1-11

<u>Mt 4:11 World English Bible Catholic Edition</u>

1 Then Jesus was led up by the Spirit into the wilderness to be tempted by the devil. 2 When he had fasted forty days and forty nights, he was hungry afterward. 3 The tempter came and said to him, "If you are the Son of God, command that these stones become bread."

4 But he answered, "It is written, 'Man shall not live by bread alone, but by every word that proceeds out of God's mouth.' "✡

5 Then the devil took him into the holy city. He set him on the pinnacle of the temple, 6 and said to him, "If you are the Son of God, throw yourself down, for it is written,

'He will command his angels concerning you,' and,

'On their hands they will bear you up,

so that you don't dash your foot against a stone.' "✡

7 Jesus said to him, "Again, it is written, 'You shall not test the Lord, your God.' "✡

*8 Again, the devil took him to an exceedingly high mountain,
and showed him all the kingdoms of the world and their glory.
9 He said to him, "I will give you all of these things, if you will
fall down and worship me."*

10 Then Jesus said to him, "Get behind me, Satan! For it is
written, 'You shall worship the Lord your God, and you shall
serve him only.'" ✡*

*11 Then the devil left him, and behold, angels came and served
him.*

In today's Gospel reading, Jesus recapitulates the stories of Noah,
and Moses, and the entire Hebrew people. Just as Noah captained his
people through forty days of flood in the ark, and Moses shepherded
his people through the forty years of the exodus from Egypt, Jesus
is shepherding us through our lives by facing his forty days in the
wilderness.

An adult life in biblical times was about forty years. For modern
people it's a bit longer, but still: over the course of our adult lives,
we live out the story told here in Matthew, this eternal, ever-repeating
journey. We weather the storms and flood waters of temptation right
along with Noah and his family. We wander through the wilderness
with Moses and the people. We walk in the wilderness with Jesus, and
we are tempted.

Try as we might, we cannot transform stones to bread. That is, we
cannot make material goods into things that nourish us. Only God
can do that. When we rightly order our lives, putting him first and
everything we do and possess in service to him and his purposes, our
stones in a sense become bread. With God, our possessions become
worthy, our food nourishes us to worthwhile activities, our
entertainment is enriched, our money serves admirable purposes, and
so on.

But if we think that even rightly ordered material goods are all we need to be fully nourished – nourished unto eternal life! – we're kidding ourselves. "Man can't live by bread alone." The wealthy are often just as miserable as the poor and starving, suffering with family discord, depression, lack of fulfillment, and so on.

And aren't those in prison well-fed? Is bread all they need? Certainly it's better to walk the straight and narrow, to work hard to feed ourselves so that we don't starve. But if we think that we can nourish our hearts, minds, and souls just by striving for material nourishment, we're doomed to unhappiness, starvation, and death – the spiritual death of separation from God.

Putting our faith in anything other than God, emotionally or physically, is like jumping from a high place and expecting to be caught. Maybe we rely on our government, leech from our parents, and borrow from our friends. Maybe we base our entire happiness on certain relationships, on our spouse or our kids. But all of those things will run their course and be gone in time. We have thrown ourselves off a high place and we are falling fast. The view is great and wind feels nice in our hair. But we are, as my mother used to say, "cruising for a bruising." Sooner or later, when we've exploited every resource and there's nothing left to hold onto, we'll hit the ground. We'll realize too late that our faith was misplaced, and that we tempted God.

The devil is a liar. Even if we worship him, we still might not get the rewards that the world has to offer. But if we worship God and God alone, we will, in the fullness of time, make it to dry land, reach the promised land, and share in the blessed hope of the resurrection.

✡4:4 Deuteronomy 8:3

  ✡4:6 Psalm 91:11-12

  ✡4:7 Deuteronomy 6:16

  *4:10 TR and NU read "Go away" instead of "Get behind me"

✡4:10 Deuteronomy 6:13

2nd Sunday of Lent, Sunday 3/5/23

Readings: Gn 12:1-4a, Ps 33:4-5, 18-19, 20, 22., 2 Tm 1:8b-10, Mt 17:1-9

<u>Mt 17:1-9 World English Bible Catholic Edition</u>

1 After six days, Jesus took with him Peter, James, and John his brother, and brought them up into a high mountain by themselves. 2 He was changed before them. His face shone like the sun, and his garments became as white as the light. 3 Behold, Moses and Elijah appeared to them talking with him.*

4 Peter answered and said to Jesus, "Lord, it is good for us to be here. If you want, let's make three tents here: one for you, one for Moses, and one for Elijah."

5 While he was still speaking, behold, a bright cloud overshadowed them. Behold, a voice came out of the cloud, saying, "This is my beloved Son, in whom I am well pleased. Listen to him."

6 When the disciples heard it, they fell on their faces, and were very afraid. 7 Jesus came and touched them and said, "Get up, and don't be afraid." 8 Lifting up their eyes, they saw no one, except Jesus alone.

9 As they were coming down from the mountain, Jesus commanded them, saying, "Don't tell anyone what you saw, until the Son of Man has risen from the dead."

The desire to categorize people, objects, and ideas is perfectly natural. To some extent at least, we all want to put things in the appropriate box. In Genesis, the first thing Adam does is name all the plants and animals. Nowadays we arrange animals into genus and species, like Homo Sapiens or Tyrannosaurus Rex. We do this because we want to know what things are, how to interact with them, and how to use them properly. We put tools on the wall of our garage in a systematic manner – screwdrivers over here, wrenches over there, and so on. We do the same with ideas – Philosophy on this side, Math on that side, Linguistics over here, etc.

Categories provide utility. Objects and ideas handily organized allow us to build things—material things, like houses, furniture, and cars, and less tangible things, like cohesive arguments, tactical plans, and systems of government. Properly categorizing things is a skill associated with high performing, successful individuals like Peter – a religious leader in charge of managing an association of apostles, and later, the nascent church.

Peter's problem in today's reading is that creating proper categories and putting them into action is easy on paper, but extremely difficult in practice. Certainly, Peter knows *intellectually* that Jesus, Moses and Elijah are in different categories, and that neither Moses nor Elijah has any need for shelter. But he still suggests building old tents. This isn't the first time that Peter has made this error. Previously, in Caesarea Philippi (Matthew 16:15-23), when Jesus asked, "But who do you say that I am?" Peter answered, "You are the Christ, the Son of the living God." Immediately afterward however, when Jesus suggests that his fate is to die, Peter strenuously objects, and Jesus says, "Get behind me, Satan!

You are a stumbling block to me, for you are not setting your mind on the things of God, but on the things of men." We shouldn't be shocked to see Peter's logic overwhelmed at the Transfiguration.

Peter's problem, which Jesus certainly understands, is a very human problem, one that all of us struggle with in everyday life. We still struggle and fail to act out the things we understand in our hearts and minds. Jesus knows how hard this is. Inside the church, we Christians are still doing it – that is, failing to behave in a manner consistent with our rules and philosophy.

And outside the faith, Jesus is often placed in the same category as Moses, Elijah, Buddha, Mohammed, Krishna, or the Dalai Lama – just another spiritual teacher. But we must get clear on this ourselves, and we must make it clear to the world.

Jesus breaks all categories. He is not like Moses. He is not like Elijah. He is in a category of One. He is God, the Creator and Logos. His words are not the words of a man. Jesus is unique. He died. He descended into hell. And on the third day, he rose again from the dead. He sits at the right hand of the father. From thence he will come to judge the quick and the dead.

*17:2 or, transfigured

3rd Sunday of Lent, Sunday 3/12/23

Readings: Ex 17:3-7, Ps 95:1-2, 6-7, 8-9, Rom 5:1-2, 5-8, Jn 4:5-42
John 4:5-42 World English Bible Catholic Edition

*So he came to a city of Samaria called Sychar, near the parcel of ground that Jacob gave to his son Joseph. 6 Jacob's well was there. Jesus therefore, being tired from his journey, sat down by the well. It was about the sixth hour.**

7 A woman of Samaria came to draw water. Jesus said to her, "Give me a drink." 8 For his disciples had gone away into the city to buy food.

9 The Samaritan woman therefore said to him, "How is it that you, being a Jew, ask for a drink from me, a Samaritan woman?" (For Jews have no dealings with Samaritans.)

10 Jesus answered her, "If you knew the gift of God, and who it is who says to you, 'Give me a drink,' you would have asked him, and he would have given you living water."

11 The woman said to him, "Sir, you have nothing to draw with, and the well is deep. So where do you get that living water? 12 Are you greater than our father Jacob, who gave us the well and drank from it himself, as did his children and his livestock?"

13 Jesus answered her, "Everyone who drinks of this water will thirst again, 14 but whoever drinks of the water that I will give him will never thirst again; but the water that I will give him will become in him a well of water springing up to eternal life."

15 The woman said to him, "Sir, give me this water, so that I don't get thirsty, neither come all the way here to draw."

16 Jesus said to her, "Go, call your husband, and come here."

17 The woman answered, "I have no husband."

Jesus said to her, "You said well, 'I have no husband,' 18 for you have had five husbands; and he whom you now have is not your husband. This you have said truly."

19 The woman said to him, "Sir, I perceive that you are a prophet. 20 Our fathers worshiped in this mountain, and you Jews say that in Jerusalem is the place where people ought to worship."

21 Jesus said to her, "Woman, believe me, the hour is coming when neither in this mountain nor in Jerusalem will you worship the Father. 22 You worship that which you don't know. We worship that which we know; for salvation is from the Jews. 23 But the hour comes, and now is, when the true worshipers will worship the Father in spirit and truth, for the Father seeks such to be his worshipers. 24 God is spirit, and those who worship him must worship in spirit and truth."

25 The woman said to him, "I know that Messiah is coming, he who is called Christ.† When he has come, he will declare to us all things."

26 Jesus said to her, "I am he, the one who speaks to you."

27 Just then, his disciples came. They marveled that he was speaking with a woman; yet no one said, "What are you looking for?" or, "Why do you speak with her?" 28 So the woman left her water pot, went away into the city, and said to the people, 29 "Come, see a man who told me everything that I have done. Can this be the Christ?" 30 They went out of the city, and were coming to him.

31 In the meanwhile, the disciples urged him, saying, "Rabbi, eat."

32 But he said to them, "I have food to eat that you don't know about."

33 The disciples therefore said to one another, "Has anyone brought him something to eat?"

34 Jesus said to them, "My food is to do the will of him who sent me and to accomplish his work. 35 Don't you say, 'There are yet four months until the harvest?' Behold, I tell you, lift up your eyes and look at the fields, that they are white for harvest already. 36 He who reaps receives wages and gathers fruit to eternal life, that both he who sows and he who reaps may rejoice together. 37 For in this the saying is true, 'One sows, and another reaps.' 38 I sent you to reap that for which you haven't labored. Others have labored, and you have entered into their labor."

39 From that city many of the Samaritans believed in him because of the word of the woman, who testified, "He told me everything that I have done." 40 So when the Samaritans came to him, they begged him to stay with them. He stayed there two

*days. 41 Many more believed because of his word. 42 They said
to the woman, "Now we believe, not because of your speaking;
for we have heard for ourselves, and know that this is indeed
the Christ, the Savior of the world."*

Brothers and sisters, last week I spoke about how Peter was overwhelmed by seeing Jesus transfigured and flanked by Moses and Elijah. Peter lost his logical and philosophical grasp on the nature of Jesus and the prophets. The great apostle offered to pitch tents for all three of them, even though Moses and Elijah, having passed on many years before, clearly had no need for tents!

This week we read the story of the Samaritan woman who, like Peter, gets confused about the nature of God and Jesus. To get down the source of her confusion, we should consider that pagan gods were tied to specific places and peoples. In those days, religion, location, and culture – food, climate, government, all of it – could not be disentangled. Caesar was a Roman god and ruler of the Roman people and the Roman empire. Egyptian pharaohs were gods, and the entire point of Egyptian religion was to maintain *maat*, the universal order that guaranteed the yearly floods which brought fertility to the Nile Delta and the Egyptian empire. Even the Jews believed that Jerusalem was the center of worship for Yahweh. Just as modern Muslims pray toward Mecca, Jews in Jesus' day prayed toward Jerusalem.

So it's not surprising that the Samaritan woman would say, *"Our fathers worshiped in this mountain, and you Jews say that in Jerusalem is the place where people ought to worship."* What's remarkable is that Jesus would reply her that that there is no single geographic place where Yahweh should be worshipped. Jesus says, *"God is spirit, and those who worship him must worship in spirit and truth."*

What is remarkable about the God of the Jews is that he is not limited by space or connected to one nation or culture like the Roman or Egyptian gods. He is the God of all who loves all.

What is remarkable is that God is not a god of nature, associated with some natural phenomena like lightning, depicted with an animal head, or associated with a planet. He is the God who *created* nature, animals, and planets.

What's remarkable is that when Moses asks for his name (Ex 3:14), God's answer isn't even a noun – it's a verb, and it's a riddle. It's usually translated as "I am who I am" but even scholars can't agree if that's correct. It has been rendered as "I am and I will be", "I am that I am", "I am what I am", "I will be what I will be", and even as "I will become what I will become."

How astonishing and remarkable that is!

People in the world today continue to struggle with the same questions and problems they struggled with in Jesus' day, although many do not know it. Consciously or unconsciously, many worship the gods of place—flags, political people, parties, and pundits—the gods of nature—environmentalism, sex, food, magic crystals—and the planetary gods of astrology and divination. And, just as the people in the biblical stories struggled, we in the church also struggle to understand, and put into practice, the meaning and implications of God and his Word.

Following in the footsteps of the woman at the well, let us have the desire embrace the message of Jesus and the implications of this unique God and Savior, and carry that message back to those in need of answers to life's most difficult questions.

4th Sunday of Lent, Sunday 3/19/23

Readings: 1 Sm 16:1b, 6-7, 10-13a, Ps 23: 1-3a, 3b-4, 5, 6, Eph 5:8-14, Jn 9:1-41

<u>John 9:1-41 World English Bible Catholic Edition</u>

1 As he passed by, he saw a man blind from birth. 2 His disciples asked him, "Rabbi, who sinned, this man or his parents, that he was born blind?"

3 Jesus answered, "This man didn't sin, nor did his parents, but that the works of God might be revealed in him. 4 I must work the works of him who sent me while it is day. The night is coming, when no one can work. 5 While I am in the world, I am the light of the world." 6 When he had said this, he spat on the ground, made mud with the saliva, anointed the blind man's eyes with the mud, 7 and said to him, "Go, wash in the pool of Siloam" (which means "Sent"). So he went away, washed, and came back seeing.

8 Therefore the neighbors and those who saw that he was blind before said, "Isn't this he who sat and begged?" 9 Others were saying, "It is he." Still others were saying, "He looks like him."

He said, "I am he."

10 They therefore were asking him, "How were your eyes opened?"

11 He answered, "A man called Jesus made mud, anointed my eyes, and said to me, 'Go to the pool of Siloam and wash.' So I went away and washed, and I received sight."

12 Then they asked him, "Where is he?"

He said, "I don't know."

13 They brought him who had been blind to the Pharisees. 14 It was a Sabbath when Jesus made the mud and opened his eyes. 15 Again therefore the Pharisees also asked him how he received his sight. He said to them, "He put mud on my eyes, I washed, and I see."

16 Some therefore of the Pharisees said, "This man is not from God, because he doesn't keep the Sabbath."

Others said, "How can a man who is a sinner do such signs?" So there was division among them.

17 Therefore they asked the blind man again, "What do you say about him, because he opened your eyes?"

He said, "He is a prophet."

18 The Jews therefore didn't believe concerning him, that he had been blind and had received his sight, until they called the parents of him who had received his sight, 19 and asked them, "Is this your son, whom you say was born blind? How then does he now see?"

20 His parents answered them, "We know that this is our son, and that he was born blind; 21 but how he now sees, we don't know; or who opened his eyes, we don't know. He is of age. Ask him. He will speak for himself." 22 His parents said these things because they feared the Jews; for the Jews had already agreed that if any man would confess him as Christ, he would be put out of the synagogue. 23 Therefore his parents said, "He is of age. Ask him."

24 So they called the man who was blind a second time, and said to him, "Give glory to God. We know that this man is a sinner."

25 He therefore answered, "I don't know if he is a sinner. One thing I do know: that though I was blind, now I see."

26 They said to him again, "What did he do to you? How did he open your eyes?"

27 He answered them, "I told you already, and you didn't listen. Why do you want to hear it again? You don't also want to become his disciples, do you?"

28 They insulted him and said, "You are his disciple, but we are disciples of Moses. 29 We know that God has spoken to Moses. But as for this man, we don't know where he comes from."

30 The man answered them, "How amazing! You don't know where he comes from, yet he opened my eyes. 31 We know that God doesn't listen to sinners, but if anyone is a worshiper of God and does his will, he listens to him. ✡ 32 Since the world began it has never been heard of that anyone opened the eyes of someone born blind. 33 If this man were not from God, he could do nothing."

34 They answered him, "You were altogether born in sins, and do you teach us?" Then they threw him out.

35 Jesus heard that they had thrown him out, and finding him, he said, "Do you believe in the Son of God?"

36 He answered, "Who is he, Lord, that I may believe in him?"

37 Jesus said to him, "You have both seen him, and it is he who speaks with you."

38 He said, "Lord, I believe!" and he worshiped him.

39 Jesus said, "I came into this world for judgment, that those who don't see may see; and that those who see may become blind."

40 Those of the Pharisees who were with him heard these things, and said to him, "Are we also blind?"

41 Jesus said to them, "If you were blind, you would have no sin; but now you say, 'We see.' Therefore your sin remains."

I love folk remedies. They've always fascinated me. Tricks like rubbing dirt on a bruise, putting butter on a burn, drinking the juice off a can of fruit for heartburn, and stopping a headache with a hot footbath. The first two don't work, by the way, but science backs up the second two. So is that what Jesus is doing in today's reading? When he makes a bit of clay from dirt and spit, is he practicing a folk remedy or perhaps casting a magic spell? No, I don't think Jesus is doing either of those things. I think he is physically illustrating or acting out an important concept.

Look at it this way. A modern businessperson illustrates sales trends using charts and graphs. A science teacher spins a small weight on a string to demonstrate centrifugal force. Actors and actresses, through plays, shows, and movie dramatizations, help us better understand complex social situations. They help us empathize with real people long after the show is over. And what Jesus does with his dramatization is blind the blind man with clay so that the Pharisees may see. Isn't that something?

Remember, the disciples asked Jesus whose sin caused the man's blindness and Jesus said nobody's sin did. Jesus knew how the Pharisees were going to react to his little reality play. So he answered the disciples, "it is so that the works of God might be made visible through him." Jesus knew that the Pharisees were blinded by their laws and rules. He knew that they would consider it impossible for a sinful man like him, who broke the sabbath rules, to perform signs – even if they saw the evidence and heard the testimony. Jesus knew that, for the Pharisees, illnesses, calamities, and catastrophes of all kinds were considered proof of sin. Therefore he knew that the Pharisees would consider the man's testimony untrustworthy because he worn blind – born in sin. And Jesus is right. When the blind man tells the Pharisees the truth of his cure, the Pharisees' answer is, "You were born totally in sin, and you are trying to teach us?" and they threw him out of their midst.

By covering the blind man's eyes with clay, Jesus shows – the same way an actor dramatizes a story—that the Pharisees *are blind to their own blindness*. Not only are they blind to the miracle Jesus has performed, they are blind to the wrong-headedness of their presuppositions.[1] And by washing away the clay to heal the man, Jesus shows that only by becoming aware of their blindness do the Pharisees have any hope of salvation. This is why Jesus said to them, "If you were blind, you would have no sin; but now you say, 'We see.' Therefore your sin remains."

The one who thinks he knows everything is closed to new knowledge. Ignorant of his own ignorance, he is blind to his own blindness and bound to remain in darkness. Only by becoming aware of our ignorance and faults can we open our eyes and move toward the light.

✡ 9:31 Psalm 66:18; Proverbs 15:29; 28:9

[1] To my knowledge this is the oldest known example of the concept, popularized in 2002 by former Secretary of Defense Donald Rumsfeld, of "unknown unknowns" – things that we do not know that we do not know. The so-called "Rumsfeld Matrix" consists of four possibilities: (1) known knowns, or things that we know and are aware of, (2) known unknowns, or things that we do not know and are fully aware that we do not know, (3) unknown unknowns, or things that we don't know that we don't know, and (4) unknown knowns, or things that we know but do not explore because they conflict with our preferred worldview. The Pharisees belong in the fourth category – the willfully blind.

5th Sunday of Lent, Sunday 3/26/23

Readings: Ez 37:12-14, Ps 130:1-2, 3-4, 5-6, 7-8, Rom 8:8-11, Jn 11:1-45

<u>John 11:1-45 World English Bible Catholic Edition</u>

1 Now a certain man was sick, Lazarus from Bethany, of the village of Mary and her sister, Martha. 2 It was that Mary who had anointed the Lord with ointment and wiped his feet with her hair, whose brother Lazarus was sick. 3 The sisters therefore sent to him, saying, "Lord, behold, he for whom you have great affection is sick."

4 But when Jesus heard it, he said, "This sickness is not to death, but for the glory of God, that God's Son may be glorified by it." 5 Now Jesus loved Martha, and her sister, and Lazarus. 6 When therefore he heard that he was sick, he stayed two days in the place where he was. 7 Then after this he said to the disciples, "Let's go into Judea again."

8 The disciples asked him, "Rabbi, the Jews were just trying to stone you. Are you going there again?"

9 Jesus answered, "Aren't there twelve hours of daylight? If a man walks in the day, he doesn't stumble, because he sees the light of this world. 10 But if a man walks in the night, he stumbles, because the light isn't in him." 11 He said these things, and after that, he said to them, "Our friend Lazarus

*has fallen asleep, but I am going so that I may awake him out
of sleep."*

*12 The disciples therefore said, "Lord, if he has fallen asleep, he
will recover."*

*13 Now Jesus had spoken of his death, but they thought that
he spoke of taking rest in sleep. 14 So Jesus said to them plainly
then, "Lazarus is dead. 15 I am glad for your sakes that I was
not there, so that you may believe. Nevertheless, let's go to him."*

16 Thomas therefore, who is called Didymus, said to his fellow
disciples, "Let's also go, that we may die with him."*

*17 So when Jesus came, he found that he had been in the
tomb four days already. 18 Now Bethany was near Jerusalem,
about fifteen stadia† away. 19 Many of the Jews had joined the
women around Martha and Mary, to console them concerning
their brother. 20 Then when Martha heard that Jesus was
coming, she went and met him, but Mary stayed in the house.
21 Therefore Martha said to Jesus, "Lord, if you would have
been here, my brother wouldn't have died. 22 Even now I know
that whatever you ask of God, God will give you."*

23 Jesus said to her, "Your brother will rise again."

*24 Martha said to him, "I know that he will rise again in the
resurrection at the last day."*

*25 Jesus said to her, "I am the resurrection and the life. He who
believes in me will still live, even if he dies. 26 Whoever lives
and believes in me will never die. Do you believe this?"*

27 She said to him, "Yes, Lord. I have come to believe that you are the Christ, God's Son, he who comes into the world."

28 When she had said this, she went away and called Mary, her sister, secretly, saying, "The Teacher is here and is calling you."

29 When she heard this, she arose quickly and went to him. 30 Now Jesus had not yet come into the village, but was in the place where Martha met him. 31 Then the Jews who were with her in the house and were consoling her, when they saw Mary, that she rose up quickly and went out, followed her, saying, "She is going to the tomb to weep there."

32 Therefore when Mary came to where Jesus was and saw him, she fell down at his feet, saying to him, "Lord, if you would have been here, my brother wouldn't have died."

33 When Jesus therefore saw her weeping, and the Jews weeping who came with her, he groaned in the spirit and was troubled, 34 and said, "Where have you laid him?"

They told him, "Lord, come and see."

35 Jesus wept.

36 The Jews therefore said, "See how much affection he had for him!" 37 Some of them said, "Couldn't this man, who opened the eyes of him who was blind, have also kept this man from dying?"

38 Jesus therefore, again groaning in himself, came to the tomb. Now it was a cave, and a stone lay against it. 39 Jesus said, "Take away the stone."

Martha, the sister of him who was dead, said to him, "Lord, by this time there is a stench, for he has been dead four days."

40 Jesus said to her, "Didn't I tell you that if you believed, you would see God's glory?"

41 So they took away the stone from the place where the dead man was lying.‡ Jesus lifted up his eyes and said, "Father, I thank you that you listened to me. 42 I know that you always listen to me, but because of the multitude standing around I said this, that they may believe that you sent me." 43 When he had said this, he cried with a loud voice, "Lazarus, come out!"

44 He who was dead came out, bound hand and foot with wrappings, and his face was wrapped around with a cloth.

Jesus said to them, "Free him, and let him go."

45 Therefore many of the Jews who came to Mary and saw what Jesus did believed in him. 46 But some of them went away to the Pharisees and told them the things which Jesus had done. 47 The chief priests therefore and the Pharisees gathered a council, and said, "What are we doing? For this man does many signs. 48 If we leave him alone like this, everyone will believe in him, and the Romans will come and take away both our place and our nation."

Brothers and sisters, we are all Lazarus. Here we are, going about our lives, making a living, grocery shopping, doing chores, paying bills, celebrating holidays, and all of the usual work-a-day things we busy ourselves with, and then – bang! – suddenly we're sick, maybe even terminally ill. And where is Jesus when we need him? Oh, he's over in the next city, out there somewhere, so far away it seems. And if we die?

Where is he then? Many are the doubters who ask, "Why would a good God let a good man die? Couldn't he just stop it?"

The scripture doesn't say what Jesus was up to that was so all-fired important that he lingered two days before heading out for Bethany to see Lazarus and his family. When we fall sick, like Lazarus, or when, like Martha and Mary, a loved one is struck down, we wonder, don't we, "What's more important than me and my family? What's the hold up?" That's just how Martha and Mary of Bethany felt. When Jesus showed up four days after their brother's death, the first thing they said was, "Lord, if you would have been here, my brother wouldn't have died." But we can't possibly know what God is up to. The tiniest corner of God's mind is beyond our comprehension. Who are we to question God?

We must have faith in the ultimate end of that plan: the blessed hope of the resurrection. Again, many are those who doubt the historicity of Lazarus's resurrection and the possibility of our resurrection in the future. Like Martha, Mary, and the rest of Lazarus' family, many grieve even though they've heard the Author of Life tell them what's to come. Why? If you believe in the Creator of the Universe, and you know the Author of Life wrote all of creation into existence out of nothing, which is the greater miracle: creating and sustaining all of existence, or raising a man from the dead? Jesus says, "Take away the stone" and Martha replies, "Lord, by this time there is a stench, for he has been dead four days." Jesus said to her, "Didn't I tell you that if you believed, you would see God's glory?" No wonder Jesus is exasperated. No wonder he, "groaned in the spirit, and was troubled." He told them in advance what he was going to do, and still they couldn't believe.

St. Paul says, "If Christ is in you, the body is dead because of sin, but the spirit is alive because of righteousness." (Rom 8:10). When we live the Christian life, guided by the Holy Spirit, God's righteousness enters us. And, despite our faults and errors, Jesus Christ loves us and weeps for us just as he loved Lazarus and wept for him outside the tomb. And that's the good news everybody – many of us stink just as badly as Lazarus did after four days in the tomb. But no matter how rotten we are, Jesus loves us just the same. No matter how bad we stink, Jesus loves us, weeps for us, and is coming for us, bringing with him the blessed hope of the resurrection.

*11:16 "Didymus" means "Twin".

†11:18 15 stadia is about 2.8 kilometers or 1.7 miles

‡11:41 NU omits "from the place where the dead man was lying."

Easter Sunday 4/9/23

Readings: Acts 10:34a, 37-43, 1 Cor 5:6b-8, Jn 20:1-9
John 20:1-9 World English Bible Catholic Edition

1 Now on the first day of the week, Mary Magdalene went early, while it was still dark, to the tomb, and saw that the stone had been taken away from the tomb. 2 Therefore she ran and came to Simon Peter and to the other disciple whom Jesus loved, and said to them, "They have taken away the Lord out of the tomb, and we don't know where they have laid him!"

3 Therefore Peter and the other disciple went out, and they went toward the tomb. 4 They both ran together. The other disciple outran Peter and came to the tomb first. 5 Stooping and looking in, he saw the linen cloths lying there; yet he didn't enter in. 6 Then Simon Peter came, following him, and entered into the tomb. He saw the linen cloths lying, 7 and the cloth that had been on his head, not lying with the linen cloths, but rolled up in a place by itself. 8 So then the other disciple who came first to the tomb also entered in, and he saw and believed. 9 For as yet they didn't know the Scripture, that he must rise from the dead.

Brothers and sisters, today I'm delivering a beautiful homily that I found in an old book entitled "Homilies Preached at Alsbury" printed for private circulation by C. Goodwin Nortion of London in 1890. The author's name is not given, may God thank and bless him. I hope you enjoy it.

"My Beloved spake unto me and said, Rise up, my love, my fair one, and come away, for lo! the winter is past, the rain is over and gone, the flowers appear on the earth, the time of the singing of birds is come, and the voice of the turtledove is heard in our land. The fig tree putteth forth her green figs, and the vines with the tender grape give a good smell. Arise, my love, my fair one, and come away."

This is the description, from the Song of Solomon, of the spring time, and of the joyousness which the flowers, and the singing of birds, and the coo of the turtle dove, and the bursting forth of the fruit-buds, produce in the hearts of those, who have passed through the winter, when all nature seems dead, and are able to rejoice at the return of spring, the foreshadowing in the natural kingdom of that time of joy and singing, when in the spiritual all things shall be made new, and all things shall be of God, when out of death life shall spring up, when light shall drive away the darkness, and the earth shall be filled with the glory of the Lord.

Do not our hearts respond to this appeal, "Arise, and come away"? Do we not hear in it a call to those, the blessed holy departed saints, who are gone into the land of forgetfulness, to prepare themselves to take again their bodies, and to burst through their cerements, to leave behind the grave-clothes, and to come forth arrayed in garments of glory and beauty, even the glory and beauty of Him, who appeared on the mount of transfiguration to the chosen disciples, His face shining as the sun, and His garment white as the light; and is it not at the same time a call to us to make ourselves ready?

The lilies, as we read, toil not neither do they spin, and the fowls of the air sow not, neither do they reap, yet our heavenly Father feedeth the fowls, and clotheth the lilies of the field, so that Solomon in all his glory was not arrayed like one of these, though they are as the grass, which grows up to-day and to-morrow is cut down and withered ; and shall He not much more clothe and feed you? We, according to these figures, are taught to give up caring for this life what we eat, and for this body what we put on in the hope of being clothed with a body of glory, and being fed with the food of eternal life, and inheriting the kingdom and glory of Christ.

We wait, in common with those of our brethren, who have fallen asleep, for the call, "Arise and come away"; we wait and embody in our daily cry to the Lord the petition for our deliverance from the bondage of corruption into liberty and glory; and in this our cry we give expression to the longing desire of those, who have gone down into silence, who have fallen asleep, who have died in the faith, not having received the promises, who wait for the time of being made perfect not without us in the glory of the resurrection.

"Christ is risen," is the song of our hearts. This day our mouth is filled with laughter, and our tongue with singing, because our captivity is at an end. If such is our experience of that salvation by hope, which we are now able to realize, what will be the joy unspeakable and full of glory which awaits us, when the day of the resurrection, to which Jesus Christ has attained, shall have come for us also? Then will be fulfilled the promise of the acceptable year of the Lord, when He shall appear again to give to them that mourn in Zion beauty for ashes, the oil of joy for mourning, the garment of praise for the spirit of heaviness.

God who is rich in mercy, when we were dead in sins, hath quickened us together with Christ, and hath raised us up together and made us sit together in the heavenlies in Christ Jesus. If we then be risen with Christ, set your affections on things above. When Christ, who is our life, shall appear again, then shall we also appear with Him in glory."

2nd Sunday of Easter, Sunday 4/16/23

Readings: Acts 2:42-47, Ps 118:2-4, 13-15, 22-24, 1 Pt 1:3-9, Jn 20:19-31

<u>John 20:19-31 World English Bible Catholic Edition</u>

When therefore it was evening on that day, the first day of the week, and when the doors were locked where the disciples were assembled, for fear of the Jews, Jesus came and stood in the middle and said to them, "Peace be to you."

20 When he had said this, he showed them his hands and his side. The disciples therefore were glad when they saw the Lord. 21 Jesus therefore said to them again, "Peace be to you. As the Father has sent me, even so I send you." 22 When he had said this, he breathed on them, and said to them, "Receive the Holy Spirit! 23 If you forgive anyone's sins, they have been forgiven them. If you retain anyone's sins, they have been retained."

24 But Thomas, one of the twelve, called Didymus,‡ wasn't with them when Jesus came. 25 The other disciples therefore said to him, "We have seen the Lord!"

But he said to them, "Unless I see in his hands the print of the nails, put my finger into the print of the nails, and put my hand into his side, I will not believe."

26 After eight days, again his disciples were inside and Thomas was with them. Jesus came, the doors being locked, and stood in the middle, and said, "Peace be to you." 27 Then he said to Thomas, "Reach here your finger, and see my hands. Reach here your hand, and put it into my side. Don't be unbelieving, but believing."

28 Thomas answered him, "My Lord and my God!"

29 Jesus said to him, "Because you have seen me,§ you have believed. Blessed are those who have not seen and have believed."

30 Therefore Jesus did many other signs in the presence of his disciples, which are not written in this book; 31 but these are written that you may believe that Jesus is the Christ, the Son of God, and that believing you may have life in his name.

For Thomas, the death and resurrection of Jesus cannot be proved except by physical evidence – placing his fingers in Jesus' wounds and putting his hand in his side. There were then, and there are now, many more men and women just like Thomas – those who need material proof in order to believe. Jesus says, *"Blessed are those who have not seen and have believed."* Indeed, blessed are they!

But the question is, where does that leave the doubting Thomases of today? What are they supposed to do with their doubts? And, when we're evangelizing, how are we supposed to answer those who say, much the same as Thomas did, "Look buddy, you're wasting your time. I'm not believing in the resurrection until I place my fingers in the wounds of his hands, and put my hand into his side." Some will even say, "Your Jesus left you high and dry – you've got no proof."

Well, I've got a very simple and direct answer that you can give to the doubting Thomases you encounter. And it goes like this.

My friend, you are not the first to want physical proof for the death and resurrection of Jesus Christ. One of his own disciples, named Thomas, when he received the news, doubted its truth until he was able to put his fingers into the wounds on Christ's hands, and place his hand into the wound where Christ was pierced by a spear. My friend, the body of Christ is alive and well, both literally and figuratively, because although Christ rose from the dead and, in a sense withdrew until he comes again, he left his mystical body, the church, "which is the blessed company of all faithful people" who are "heirs through hope" of his "everlasting kingdom" (BCP 1928). We invite you, dear brother, to put your hand in our hand and to feel our wounds, and to place your hand into our side, and let us show you the reality of Christ. "For even as we have many members" we "who are many, are one body in Christ, and individually members of one another" (Rom 12:4-5).

This is not a metaphor, my dear doubting friend. Nor are these just some clever words. Christians have believed from the earliest days of the church, that all believers taken together are the literal body of Christ on earth and have used that precise term. Christ knew this moment would come, and he left his body, the church, right here on earth so that you could test, and see, and have proof.

Many of us have been like you, alienated or even enemies of God, separated from him by doubts, misapprehensions, delusions, and immaturity. Many of us have been swayed by convincing skeptics, witty cynics, and naysayers. But "don't let anyone rob you through philosophy and vain deceit, after the tradition of men, and the rudiments of the world" from being made full. "For in him all the fullness of the Deity dwells bodily, and in him you are made full, who is the head of all principality and power." (Col 2:8-10). The doors are open my friend. Come inside, put your hand in ours, test and see for yourself the fullness, happiness, healing, forgiveness, and salvation that await you inside the body of Christ.

This is the good news we must share, brothers and sisters, with the doubting Thomases of this world.

‡ 20:24 or, Twin
    § 20:29 TR adds "Thomas,"

3rd Sunday of Easter, Sunday 4/23/23

Readings: Acts 2:14, 22-33, Ps 16:1-2, 5, 7-8, 9-10, 11, 1 Pt 1:17-21, Lk 24:13-35

<u>Luke 24:13-25 World English Bible Catholic Edition</u>

13 Behold, two of them were going that very day to a village named Emmaus, which was sixty stadia from Jerusalem. 14 They talked with each other about all of these things which had happened. 15 While they talked and questioned together, Jesus himself came near, and went with them. 16 But their eyes were kept from recognizing him. 17 He said to them, "What are you talking about as you walk, and are sad?"*

18 One of them, named Cleopas, answered him, "Are you the only stranger in Jerusalem who doesn't know the things which have happened there in these days?"

19 He said to them, "What things?"

They said to him, "The things concerning Jesus the Nazarene, who was a prophet mighty in deed and word before God and all the people; 20 and how the chief priests and our rulers delivered him up to be condemned to death, and crucified him. 21 But we were hoping that it was he who would redeem Israel. Yes, and besides all this, it is now the third day since these things happened. 22 Also, certain women of our company amazed us, having arrived early at the tomb; 23 and when they didn't find his body, they came saying that they had also seen a vision of angels, who said that he was alive. 24 Some of us went to the tomb and found it just like the women had said, but they didn't see him."

25 He said to them, "Foolish people, and slow of heart to believe in all that the prophets have spoken! 26 Didn't the Christ have to suffer these things and to enter into his glory?" 27 Beginning from Moses and from all the prophets, he explained to them in all the Scriptures the things concerning himself.

28 They came near to the village where they were going, and he acted like he would go further.

29 They urged him, saying, "Stay with us, for it is almost evening, and the day is almost over."

He went in to stay with them. 30 When he had sat down at the table with them, he took the bread and gave thanks. Breaking it, he gave it to them. 31 Their eyes were opened and they recognized him; then he vanished out of their sight. 32 They said to one another, "Weren't our hearts burning within us while he spoke to us along the way, and while he opened the Scriptures to us?" 33 They rose up that very hour, returned to Jerusalem, and found the eleven gathered together, and those who were with them, 34 saying, "The Lord is risen indeed, and has appeared to Simon!" 35 They related the things that happened along the way, and how he was recognized by them in the breaking of the bread.

Brothers and sisters, in today's Gospel reading we meet two disciples leaving Jerusalem in sadness, headed the wrong way. Incredible things have happened and continued to happen, but they're leaving the

Holy City. If this were a movie, we'd be yelling at the screen, "turn around, go back, you're missing everything!" But you see, they hadn't seen the meaning in the prophecies and in Jesus' teaching. They had been sent into a tailspin by his death on a cross. They were, in a sense, lost.

Isn't that what this culture, this nation, is doing? Going in the wrong direction? Failing to see the meaning of the scriptures? Failing to understand the prophecies? Each year in the U.S. fifteen hundred churches shut their doors forever. We too are headed away from Jerusalem, running from the truth.

But Jesus was with the disciple Cleopas and his companion, right there in their midst, his identity unrecognized. Jesus asks them to recount the events that had taken place, and to explain why they're sad, and they do. They know everything. They have their facts straight and they can relate the proceedings perfectly. But, as we know, there is no meaning inherent in facts. Knowing facts is mere knowledge; *wisdom is knowing what to do*. And so Jesus illuminates the events, the scriptures, and prophecies to them in such a way they begin to understand. They ask for more. When he appears to them in the breaking of the bread, it all comes together for them. They get beyond the mere facts and receive wisdom—that is, they begin to know what they must do. They immediately change direction. They head back to the Holy City of Jerusalem to rejoin the other disciples.

This culture also knows the facts. The facts are all over the news! We're in the midst of a mental health crisis. The demons of depression, addiction, apathy, and hopelessness drive 1.2 million people each year to attempt suicide in our country – about one-in-five of them teens – a 50% increase in the last twenty years. Over 100,000 died from overdoses last year, five times more than just twenty years ago. Just like Cleopas and his fellow disciple, this culture knows the facts, but it doesn't see the *meaning*. Jesus is walking among us *right now*. But we don't engage with him, we don't have dialogue with him. We don't allow him to show us the meaning beyond the facts and the data. And so, this culture continues to flounder. It lacks wisdom. *It has no idea what to do.*

The good news is this, everybody. It's what Jesus spoke to us when he was mercilessly nailed to the cross, as we read in Luke 23:34: "Father forgive them, for they know not what they do." Jesus Christ is well aware that this culture and this nation knows not what it is doing. Ignorance, according to Jesus, is a valid excuse. He forgives us, even as he forgave those who crucified him.

There is still time to engage with him in dialogue. To listen. To accept his wisdom. To change direction and return to the Holy City.

* 24:13 60 stadia = about 11 kilometers or about 7 miles.

4th Sunday of Easter, Sunday 4/30/23

Readings: Acts 2:14a, 36-41, Ps 23: 1-3a, 3b4, 5, 6, 1 Pt 2:20b-25, Jn 10:1-10

John 10:1-10 World English Bible Catholic Edition

1 "Most certainly, I tell you, one who doesn't enter by the door into the sheep fold, but climbs up some other way, is a thief and a robber. 2 But one who enters in by the door is the shepherd of the sheep. 3 The gatekeeper opens the gate for him, and the sheep listen to his voice. He calls his own sheep by name and leads them out. 4 Whenever he brings out his own sheep, he goes before them; and the sheep follow him, for they know his voice. 5 They will by no means follow a stranger, but will flee from him; for they don't know the voice of strangers." 6 Jesus spoke this parable to them, but they didn't understand what he was telling them.

7 Jesus therefore said to them again, "Most certainly, I tell you, I am the sheep's door. 8 All who came before me are thieves and robbers, but the sheep didn't listen to them. 9 I am the door. If anyone enters in by me, he will be saved, and will go in and go out and will find pasture. 10 The thief only comes to steal, kill, and destroy. I came that they may have life, and may have it abundantly.

Brothers and sisters, Jesus Christ is the Good Shepherd, and the good shepherd doesn't force, threaten, or frighten the sheep. This is a widely known leadership philosophy, one that has been attributed to everyone from Gen. George S. Patton to economist Maynard Keynes. I'm not sure who said it first, but it goes like this: "People are like rope. You can pull them, but you can't push them."†

Jesus says, "The gatekeeper opens the gate for him, and the sheep listen to his voice." A good shepherd pulls and leads the sheep. He has a *relationship* with the sheep. Look at it this way. A gate is a line of defense. When we push people, they get defensive. The gates, as it were, are closed and locked. But if we lead, inspire, and have a relationship with people, their defenses naturally open and they follow us.

The sheep follow the good shepherd because they "know his voice" and "will by no means follow a stranger but will flee from him." Unlike Jesus, the Pharisees, push. They don't care about the defensive feelings of the people. They force behavior by punishing lawbreakers. Rather than loving the people as a good shepherd loves his sheep, they objectify the people, treating them like defendants in the legal framework of Hebraic law's 613 commandments.

All of this was on display in the previous episode in the Gospel of John. Remember how the Pharisees were up in arms about Jesus' healing of the blind man on the sabbath? Remember how they dragged the blind man into court – twice! – and then his family as well? This is precisely what Jesus is talking about.

The thief and the bandit get what they want at the point of a weapon. The robber says, "Give me all your money!" A bad leader is like a robber. Instead of demanding money or goods, a bad leader says, "Obey the rules or you will be punished!" When Jesus says, "All who came before me are thieves and robbers" it is a bold and revolutionary statement! All of the previous prophets – all of the leaders, teachers, and kings of the Hebrews – were pushing. Unlike Jesus, they used threats and punishments to try and impose good behavior.

Jesus still wants us to follow the rules – to obey the ten commandments, say our prayers, observe the holidays, participate in church rituals, and so on – but not out of fear. He wants us to do it voluntarily, organically, from a place of love and inspiration. He says, "The thief only comes to steal, kill, and destroy. I came that they may have life, and may have it abundantly." He wants to come with him willingly, freely, and joyfully, and live with him in eternal life!

† Those who are interested in this concept from a sociological, governmental, and/or business perspective should research the term "enforcement cost." The emotional, operational, and efficiency costs of excessive policies and procedures – a.k.a. "red tape" – is a massive drain on companies. The fiscal costs of policing and litigation crushes societies and governments. Examples are everywhere. Getting people to cooperate and do things properly of their own accord saves individuals, communities, businesses and governments trillions of dollars – and makes folks happier to boot!

5th Sunday of Easter, Sunday 5/7/23

Readings: Acts 6:1-7, Ps 33:1-2, 4-5, 18-19, 1 Pt 2:4-9, Jn 14:1-12
John 14:1-12 World English Bible Catholic Edition

1 "Don't let your heart be troubled. Believe in God. Believe also in me. 2 In my Father's house are many homes. If it weren't so, I would have told you. I am going to prepare a place for you. 3 If I go and prepare a place for you, I will come again and will receive you to myself; that where I am, you may be there also. 4 You know where I go, and you know the way."

5 Thomas said to him, "Lord, we don't know where you are going. How can we know the way?"

6 Jesus said to him, "I am the way, the truth, and the life. No one comes to the Father, except through me. 7 If you had known me, you would have known my Father also. From now on, you know him and have seen him."

8 Philip said to him, "Lord, show us the Father, and that will be enough for us."

9 Jesus said to him, "Have I been with you such a long time, and do you not know me, Philip? He who has seen me has seen the Father. How do you say, 'Show us the Father?' 10 Don't you believe that I am in the Father, and the Father in me? The words that I tell you, I speak not from myself; but the Father who lives in me does his works. 11 Believe me that I am in the Father, and the Father in me; or else believe me for the very works' sake. 12 Most certainly I tell you, he who believes in me, the works that I do, he will do also; and he will do greater works than these, because I am going to my Father.

In the passage prior to today's reading (John 13:36-38), Jesus says to his apostles, "Where I am going, you can't follow now, but you will follow afterwards." Simon Peter says he will lay down his life in order to follow, but Jesus foretells that Simon will instead deny him three times.

This is why Jesus says in today's reading, "Don't let your heart be troubled. Believe in God. Believe also in me. In my Father's house are many homes." Jesus is consoling Peter and the apostles for the mistakes he knows they are going to make. A home is a place to feel comfortable and safe. A home is a place of refuge for individuals and families. "In my Father's house are many homes." Pardon the pun, but this very much sounds like, "Don't dwell on the past – dwell with Jesus and the Father in the home prepared for you. There's plenty of room."

Jesus warns Peter – he warns us! – that we're going to stumble. In our reading from 1 Peter, we hear "The stone that the builders rejected has become the cornerstone, and a stone that will make people stumble, and a rock that will make them fall. They stumble by disobeying the word, as is their destiny." Yes, we're going to stumble. But there's a home waiting for us. A home is a place of recuperation and rest after a long day of struggle, trial, tribulation, and hard work. After a lifetime of hard work trying to follow Jesus, after a lifetime of stumbling, fumbling, and failing, there is a home waiting for us where we can rest our weary bones.

Like Simon Peter, I have denied Jesus many times in my life. I have run from his truth, tried to justify my bad behavior, deliberately disobeyed his teachings, and so on. I cringe and shrink away from the memories of my misdeeds. We have all done this to one degree or the other. That's why, to some extent, we can all imagine the guilt and shame Simon Peter must've felt after denying the Lord three times, only to meet his beloved Lord face to face after the resurrection.

As St. Augustine of Hippo said in his <u>Confessions</u>, "You have made us for yourself, O Lord, and our heart is restless until it rests in you." So, not only is rest available to us in God's house in the future, but rest is also available today if only we will stop running from God. We struggle, deny, and stumble. We fall. We get up again. On we go. But let us not be restless or troubled. Let us instead follow Jesus Christ and find our rest through him, with him and in him, today, tomorrow, and for eternity.

6th Sunday of Easter, Sunday 5/14/23

Readings: Acts 8:5-8, 14-17, Ps 66:1-3, 4-5, 6-7, 16, 20, 1 Pt 3:15-18, Jn 14:15-21

<u>John 14:15-21 World English Bible</u>

Jesus said, "If you love me, keep my commandments. 16 I will pray to the Father, and he will give you another Counselor, † that he may be with you forever: 17 the Spirit of truth, whom the world can't receive, for it doesn't see him and doesn't know him. You know him, for he lives with you and will be in you. 18 I will not leave you orphans. I will come to you. 19 Yet a little while, and the world will see me no more; but you will see me. Because I live, you will live also. 20 In that day you will know that I am in my Father, and you in me, and I in you. 21 One who has my commandments and keeps them, that person is one who loves me. One who loves me will be loved by my Father, and I will love him, and will reveal myself to him."

In today's reading Jesus informs his apostles that, although he is leaving the world, Heavenly Father is going send to them a counselor and guide to be with them forever. Nowadays the preferred term for this counselor is the "Holy Spirit."

I confess without shame that I prefer the older term "Holy Ghost." Is it partly nostalgic? An appreciation for antique words? Maybe a little. But mainly, I prefer to say "Holy Ghost" for exactly the same reason that most people *don't* like it: because "Holy Ghost" sounds strange, bizarre, and just a little bit creepy. It sounds different.

And the Holy Ghost should sound different. In the minds of most young people today, Christianity is just another hobby, one choice among a host of various spiritual pursuits. These days, spirituality is about feeling good, recharging your batteries, and maximizing your happiness and productivity. And as far as the youth of today are concerned, there are lots of ways to be spiritual. To them, being filled with the Holy Spirit is roughly the same as the refreshing, vaguely spiritual feeling you get after a really good massage with healing herbs, or an aromatherapy session.

The words "spirit" and "spirituality" are severely over-used and tossed around lightly. There are all kinds of "spirit." A medium can claim to call upon the spirits. A high school can have team spirit. An army can cultivate fighting spirit. The word "spirit" is vague. "Holy Ghost" is specific.

There is only one Holy Ghost.

The Holy Ghost is, like Christian spirituality, unique. When you reference the Holy Ghost, it's clear you are not talking about anything else. This isn't just another type of spirituality, like yoga, mindfulness, Reiki, or Transcendental Meditation. We are dealing with an entity, a power, something completely *other*. So yes, the term "Holy Ghost" sounds weird, different, shocking. This culture desperately needs to be shocked—shocked out of complacency, shocked out of folly, foolishness, and faithlessness – and reminded that Christianity is not a product. The Holy Trinity is not for sale. God is not a brand name, Jesus has no equivalents, and the Holy Ghost has no competitors.

This week the Surgeon General of the United States published his 82-page report entitled "Our Epidemic of Loneliness and Isolation[1]." It reveals that half of Americans are suffering from the negative health effects of loneliness, which are the rough equivalent of smoking 15

---

1.   https://www.hhs.gov/sites/default/files/surgeon-general-social-connection-advisory.pdf

cigarettes a day – more severe than obesity and lack of exercise. Meanwhile, the facilities that have the cure for this epidemic – America's churches! – are closing at the rate of five per day.

It's past time we made it absolutely clear that what we are offering to this suffering culture is something entirely different. We are the Body of Christ, his church, filled with the Holy Ghost! Inside these doors, you may eat the flesh and drink the blood of God. With him, and through him, and in him, you can be possessed by the Holy Ghost, remake yourself completely, and find peace in the blessed hope of life everlasting!

That's the power of the Holy Ghost. And you can't get that from your masseuse, or your yoga teacher, or your mindfulness coach.

† 14:16 Greek παρακλητον: Counselor, Helper, Intercessor, Advocate, and Comforter.

The Ascension of the Lord, Sunday 5/21/23

Readings: Acts 1:1-11, Ps 47:2-3, 6-7, 8-9, Eph 1:17-23, Mt 28:16-20

Matthew 28:16-20 World English Bible Catholic Edition

16 But the eleven disciples went into Galilee, to the mountain where Jesus had sent them. 17 When they saw him, they bowed down to him; but some doubted. 18 Jesus came to them and spoke to them, saying, "All authority has been given to me in heaven and on earth. 19 Go‡ and make disciples of all nations, baptizing them in the name of the Father and of the Son and of the Holy Spirit, 20 teaching them to observe all things that I commanded you. Behold, I am with you always, even to the end of the age." Amen.

Brothers and sisters, we read in todays Gospel that, when Jesus appeared to the eleven disciples on the Mount of Olives, "they saw him and bowed down to him; but some doubted." What were they doubting? Weren't they seeing him, the risen Christ, in the flesh?

Is it possible they were doubting their eyes, or their own thought processes, their own logic? A wise man looks twice, knowing that at first glance he sees what he wishes to see. Is it possible that the Gospel is conveying a sort of double-take on the part of a few of the disciples? Some biblical scholars suggest that the word "doubt" would be better understood as "hesitancy," meaning that some of the disciples were uncertain as they bowed down and worshiped him. Possible? Maybe.

But doesn't it make more sense that they were doubting, not Jesus Christ, but themselves? Doesn't it make more sense that they were hesitant about their mission, that is, going forward to do their work without Jesus being present in the manner he was previously? Some degree of doubt and hesitancy would be understandable, wouldn't it, given the astounding nature of what they were witnessing, and the impossible mission they were given? Of course it would. Afterall, the disciples didn't know what we know now.

Even though we weren't there to see and sit with the risen Jesus Christ, we need not have any doubt or hesitancy because we know that the Ascension of Christ was real. We are witnesses to the Ascension of Christ. We know that the obscure teachings of Jesus of Nazareth rose to ascendancy in the hierarchy of ideas. Respect for human rights, and the inherent value of human life, largely unheard of in the ancient world, are now a primary concern nationally and internationally. Charity and public service, rarities in the time of Jesus, are now commonplace practices. We know that the disciples did exactly what Jesus Christ commanded them to do – that they went forth to "make disciples of all nations, baptizing them in the name of the Father and of the Son and of the Holy Spirit." We know Christianity grew from a small Jewish sect into the world's majority religion.

We need have no doubts or hesitancy because we've seen that, although he withdrew from physical view, Jesus Christ became a beacon to the world. In the same way that a kite becomes visible to more and more observers the higher it rises, the Creator and Logos has ascended to very high place in human culture. This is both an observable fact and a continuing, aeternal † process that surpasses the merely temporal, physical, and material.

Jesus Christ withdrew from a world of limitations and ascended to heaven, a place of limitless potential. The Ascension was, is, and always will be happening. It began before the foundation of the world and continues now through our participation. So let us go out and, armed with knowledge the eleven themselves did not have, and participate in the continuing Ascension of Christ. Let us elevate him still higher in the eyes of all humanity, lifting him up to the highest place for all to see and worship.

‡ 28:19 TR and NU add "therefore"

† Here I use the archaic spelling *aeternal* to describe something that is not bound by the limits of time.

Homily for Pentecost Sunday 5/28/23

Readings: Acts 2:1-11, 104:1, 24, 29-30, 31, 34, 1 Cor 12:3b-7, 12-13, Veni, Sancte Spiritus, Jn 20:19-23

<u>Acts 2:1-11 World English Bible Catholic Edition</u>

1 Now when the day of Pentecost had come, they were all with one accord in one place. 2 Suddenly there came from the sky a sound like the rushing of a mighty wind, and it filled all the house where they were sitting. 3 Tongues like fire appeared and were distributed to them, and one sat on each of them. 4 They were all filled with the Holy Spirit and began to speak with other languages, as the Spirit gave them the ability to speak.

5 Now there were dwelling in Jerusalem Jews, devout men, from every nation under the sky. 6 When this sound was heard, the multitude came together and were bewildered, because everyone heard them speaking in his own language. 7 They were all amazed and marveled, saying to one another, "Behold, aren't all these who speak Galileans? 8 How do we hear, everyone in our own native language? 9 Parthians, Medes, Elamites, and people from Mesopotamia, Judea, Cappadocia, Pontus, Asia, 10 Phrygia, Pamphylia, Egypt, the parts of Libya around Cyrene, visitors from Rome, both Jews and proselytes, 11 Cretans and Arabians—we hear them speaking in our languages the mighty works of God!"

Flame? Tongues of fire? Tongues of fire that came down to rest on each of the disciples? What is this flame that gives them the ability to communicate with people of all cultures and fills them with miraculous energy, dedication, drive, and fearlessness, such that they willing and able to stand up to persecution, torture, and execution to spread the message?

This is the same flame that set a bush alight without consuming it, drew Moses aside from his path, and signaled that he must take on a new life's mission – to lead his people out of bondage.

This is the same flame that, after the people have escaped Egyptian tyranny, appears as a pillar of fire to lead them through the wilderness by night. In Deut 4:24 we read, "Our God is a consuming fire." And Isaiah declares,

> *Who among us can live with the devouring fire?*
> *Who among us can live with everlasting burning?*
> *He who walks righteously*
> *and speaks blamelessly,*
> *he who despises the gain of oppressions,*
> *who gestures with his hands, refusing to take a bribe,*
> *who stops his ears from hearing of bloodshed,*
> *and shuts his eyes from looking at evil –*
> *he will dwell on high.* (Isa 33:14b-16a)

This is the flame that does not consume our flesh but, if we allow it, burns away our desire to sin and shows us a way through the darkness we encounter in daily life.

This is the flame that burns away our appetite for money, power, and fame, and lights us up with passion to do God's work.

This is the fire that, as we try to walk in the footsteps of Jesus Christ, burns away the dead wood, and renews the forest of our heart, mind, and soul.

This is the flame that so purified and illuminated St. Paul that he was able to proclaim, "I have been crucified with Christ. It is no longer I who live but Christ who lives in me." (Gal 2:20)

This is the fire of the Holy Ghost. Let us all, my brothers and sisters, burn with this fire. Let us give our lives to Christ and proclaim him to the nations as the disciples did. And let us all pray, as the priest does in Mass after he has incensed the altar, "May the Lord enkindle within us the fire of His love and the flame of everlasting charity."

Homily for Trinity Sunday 6/4/23

Readings: Ex 34:4b-6, 8-9, Dn 3:52, 53, 54, 55, 56, 2 Cor 13:11-13, Jn 3:16-18

<u>John 3:16-18 World English Bible Catholic Edition</u>

16 For God so loved the world, that he gave his only born§ Son, that whoever believes in him should not perish, but have eternal life. 17 For God didn't send his Son into the world to judge the world, but that the world should be saved through him. 18 He who believes in him is not judged. He who doesn't believe has been judged already, because he has not believed in the name of the only born Son of God.

All sin, as St. Augustine said, is "incurvatus in se" – to be curved inward on oneself. Not expanding outward to fulfill one's proper role in the family, the community, the nation, and the world, but collapsed inwardly. The seven deadly sins manifest this truth. Pride is the mirror that says we are the loveliest of all, and envy is the one that says we are not, but we should be. Greed and lust are obsessions with obtaining our desires. Wrath is about exerting our will, and sloth is disregard for our duties to others.

The opposite of curving inward is to give of oneself, which God embodies in his trinitarian structure. In his role as the source and establisher of creation, God is the sheer act of being itself. God could have remained inward, a single point, complete in himself. But in his goodness, for our benefit, he looked out upon the void, imagined reality itself, and spoke it into being.

And then we, humanity, curved inward on ourselves. The church fathers agree that the apple would have been ours eventually, when we were ready. But Adam and Eve, our first parents, weren't concerned with God's plan or the fate of their descendants. No, they were thinking only of their immediate wants and desires. They could have expanded outside themselves to fill up their role in God's creation. But instead, concerned with their own will, they grasped rather than waiting to be offered, and collapsed inwardly into sin. And that's the way it has mostly been with the human family ever since.

Yet God, ever-loving, ever-forgiving, ever-expansive, sent his only begotten son, Jesus Christ, down into our sin to pull us out. Again, God could've remained a single, fixed point, being complete as he truly is, in and of himself. But no – he deigned to grant us a second point of contact. He came down and offered himself up in total sacrifice to show us the way out of the inward-curving, downward spiral we created.

This act of complete sacrifice and love we repaid by killing him on a cross. Did God withdraw? Did he become angry, and disdain his creation? No, he went further still. Our ever-forgiving, ever-loving God gave even more. He gifted us a third point of connection, the Holy Ghost, to be with us always and show us the way.

Today, brothers and sisters, let us with one voice celebrate and praise the Holy Trinity. Let us embrace him as our Holy Father, who rightly and sweetly ordered all things, who gave us rules and structure, laws of physics, morality, and ethics. Let us accept his son Jesus Christ, our Lord and Savior, the Logos, whose loving hands created meaning itself and reached down into our sin to drag us upward into eternal life. Let us burn with the fire of God's Holy Ghost and embody his goodness and truth.

Let us not grasp, hold, and curve inwardly, but live by God's example and forgive, freely give, and empty ourselves out into the world.

The Feast of Corpus Christi, Sunday 6/11/23

Readings: Dt 8:2-3, 14b-16a, Ps 147:12-13, 14-15, 19-20, 1 Cor 10:16-17, Jn 6:51-58

<u>John 6:51-58 World English Bible Catholic Edition</u>

Jesus said, 51 I am the living bread which came down out of heaven. If anyone eats of this bread, he will live forever. Yes, the bread which I will give for the life of the world is my flesh."

52 The Jews therefore contended with one another, saying, "How can this man give us his flesh to eat?"

53 Jesus therefore said to them, "Most certainly I tell you, unless you eat the flesh of the Son of Man and drink his blood, you don't have life in yourselves. 54 He who eats my flesh and drinks my blood has eternal life, and I will raise him up at the last day. 55 For my flesh is food indeed, and my blood is drink indeed. 56 He who eats my flesh and drinks my blood lives in me, and I in him. 57 As the living Father sent me, and I live because of the Father, so he who feeds on me will also live because of me. 58 This is the bread which came down out of heaven—not as our fathers ate the manna and died. He who eats this bread will live forever."

These days most folks seem to believe humanity can nourish itself. Afterall, we grow food and raise livestock on industrial farms, don't we? And, thanks to innovations in agriculture, improvements in financial markets, advances in international relations, and the retreat of communism, we have raised more people out of poverty and starvation in the last 20 years than we did in the previous 200 years.

And, fewer people are dying by violence in this century than in the last. Owing to the collapse of socialist regimes like Germany's Third Reich and the U.S.S.R., and owing to capitalist reforms in China, fewer people are dying by violence in this century than in the last.

On the medical front, human life expectancy continues to increase. More and more diseases are being pushed back with new medications and treatments. And somehow, despite disagreement and contentiousness about the right policies and treatments, we were able to overcome a worldwide pandemic with far fewer casualties than projected.

So, at first glance, humanity seems to have things under control. But the exact opposite is true. Monsanto can genetically engineer drought-resistant crop seeds, but only God can send down the sun and rain to raise corn from seed to ear. Only God holds the key to the mystery of germination. We can create antibiotics, medications, and technologies to improve the yield of livestock farms, but only God can breathe life into a newborn calf, or stir the tiny heart of a chick to peck its way from the shell. Scientists and doctors can engineer new treatments to support the body, but in the end, the human body always heals itself by the miracle of God's curative process.

And just because we've decided to take a break from the slaughter of the last century – two worldwide wars, a genocide, and a half-dozen communist purges – doesn't mean that we can nourish ourselves morally and ethically. There's a war going on right now in Ukraine. Political polarization is at an all-time high in the U.S. and in Europe. Make no mistake: one match could once again set the world ablaze. We could quickly return to the desert of famine, poverty, war, and disease. We could once again be like the Hebrews following Moses into the desert, fleeing Egyptian tyranny and searching for the promised land. When they hungered and thirsted for physical, moral, and spiritual nourishment, God send manna from heaven like the dewfall so that the people could gather it each morning and live. But that bread, miraculous though it was, was but a dim foreshadowing of Jesus Christ to come.

Today, as we celebrate the Feast of Corpus Christi, the Body and Blood of Christ, let's remind ourselves, and our fellow man, that we cannot nourish ourselves physically, morally, or spiritually. Let's proclaim to the world that, "Blessed are those who hunger and thirst for righteousness, for they shall be filled" (Matt 5:6); that all physical sustenance is a biological miracle that comes from God; that morality itself emerges from God because God is Love, and the fullness of spiritual nourishment lies in the living bread that came down from heaven, our Lord Jesus Christ.

11th Sunday of Ordinary Time, Sunday 6/18/23

Readings: Ex 19:2-6a, Ps 100:1-2, 3, 5, Romans 5:6-11, Matthew 9:36—10:8

<u>Matthew 9:36—10:8 World English Bible Catholic Edition</u>

36 But when he saw the multitudes, he was moved with compassion for them because they were harassed§ and scattered, like sheep without a shepherd. 37 Then he said to his disciples, "The harvest indeed is plentiful, but the laborers are few. 38 Pray therefore that the Lord of the harvest will send out laborers into his harvest."

1 He called to himself his twelve disciples, and gave them authority over unclean spirits, to cast them out, and to heal every disease and every sickness. 2 Now the names of the twelve apostles are these. The first, Simon, who is called Peter; Andrew, his brother; James the son of Zebedee; John, his brother; 3 Philip; Bartholomew; Thomas; Matthew the tax collector; James the son of Alphaeus; Lebbaeus, who was also called† Thaddaeus; 4 Simon the Zealot; and Judas Iscariot, who also betrayed him.

5 Jesus sent these twelve out and commanded them, saying, "Don't go among the Gentiles, and don't enter into any city of

*the Samaritans. 6 Rather, go to the lost sheep of the house of
Israel. 7 As you go, preach, saying, 'The Kingdom of Heaven
is at hand!' 8 Heal the sick, cleanse the lepers,‡ and cast out
demons. Freely you received, so freely give.*

Brothers and sisters, this week we have no holiday, no solemnity, and no feast. It's not Easter, or Christmas, or any of that. And yet in this week's readings we find a message that is one of the most profound and important in all the Gospel.

In our reading of Romans 5:6-11, Paul says, "God commends his own love toward us, in that while we were yet sinners, Christ died for us." And then he adds, "For if while we were enemies, we were reconciled to God through the death of his Son, much more, being reconciled, we will be saved by his life." He's saying in essence, "If you think Christ's Passion reconciled you to God, you ain't seen nothing yet – wait until you see what comes with accepting Christ's Resurrection!"

Imagine if we allowed ourselves to be crucified and resurrected in Christ. What might we be capable of? What might we be able to achieve? We might be able to become "a kingdom of priests and a holy nation" as we heard in our first reading from Exodus. It might even be possible for us to go forth, as the disciples are charged to do in today's Gospel reading, to "heal the sick, raise the dead, cleanse the lepers, and cast out demons" – freely giving as we freely received.

Why freely giving? Because Christ freely gave his life for us. And also because, as Ezekiel says (Ez 17:24), it is the Lord who brings low the high tree and lifts up the low tree; who withers up the green tree and makes the withered tree bloom. It is God who decides who is blessed and who is damned, who will wither in the wilderness of falsehood and who will take root and blossom in his truth. And so, it's not for us to decide to whom we should or should not freely give our love.

Next Saturday, June 24th, 2023 on the Feast of the Solemnity of St. John the Baptist, I will be vested as a priest. During the final class I'm required to take in preparation for the service, Father Clyde Kuemmerle told us that in the old days, priests walked their parishes frequently, speaking to everyone they met, getting to know each and every neighbor, offering help and assistance to baptized and unbaptized alike. He said that we would do well to emulate the old ways.

And that's great advice, not just for aspiring priests, but for us all. Each and every one of us should strive to be a priest, and everyone we meet should be our neighbor. And let's not forget that our assignment is to love our neighbor as ourselves (Mt 22:39-40).

§ 9:36 TR reads "weary" instead of "harassed"

    † 10:3 NU omits "Lebbaeus, who was also called"

    ‡ 10:8 TR adds "raise the dead,"

12th Sunday of Ordinary Time, Sunday 6/25/23

Readings: Jer 20:10-13, Ps 69:8-10, 14, 17, 33-35, Rom 5:12-15, Mt 10:26-33

<u>Matthew 10:26—33 World English Bible Catholic Edition</u>

26 Therefore don't be afraid of them, for there is nothing covered that will not be revealed, or hidden that will not be known. 27 What I tell you in the darkness, speak in the light; and what you hear whispered in the ear, proclaim on the housetops. 28 Don't be afraid of those who kill the body, but are not able to kill the soul. Rather, fear him who is able to destroy both soul and body in Gehenna.†

29 "Aren't two sparrows sold for an assarion coin?‡ Not one of them falls to the ground apart from your Father's will. 30 But the very hairs of your head are all numbered. 31 Therefore don't be afraid. You are of more value than many sparrows. 32 Everyone therefore who confesses me before men, I will also confess him before my Father who is in heaven. 33 But whoever denies me before men, I will also deny him before my Father who is in heaven.

Brothers and sisters, Truth, along with Goodness and Beauty, is one of the three transcendentals. The transcendentals are the three irreducible qualities. Think of it this way. Most numbers can be evenly divided, like 16 let's say, into 2-times-8, or 4-times-4. Qualities are the same way. Patriotism, for example, can be divided into constituent parts. It's made up of love of country, military service, civil service, philosophical and cultural aspects, defense of shared values, and so on. Just as there are prime numbers that cannot be evenly reduced – like 1, 3, 5, 7, 11, etc. – the transcendental qualities cannot be reduced any further either. According to the Catechism of the Catholic Church, we can't conceive of God's infinite perfection. But we can see a reflection his perfection in the three irreducible transcendentals when they manifest in his creatures:

> 41 All creatures bear a certain resemblance to God, most especially man, created in the image and likeness of God. The manifold perfections of creatures - their truth, their goodness, their beauty all reflect the infinite perfection of God. *

So, in a sense, whenever we see Truth, Goodness, and Beauty in God's creation, we see his fingerprints.

The power of Truth is in the forefront of today's Gospel reading, which reminds us that speaking the truth is essential. Look, we're not perfect. It's difficult to communicate with others when we're being honest and kind. But if we twist facts, hide motives, and behave inconsiderately, communication is downright impossible. Without truth, communication is doomed. When I mentor people in the business world who aspire to be managers, I stress the importance of truth in all they do. I often say, "Your success as a manager is directly proportional to your ability to express the truth with kindness, diplomacy, and tact." Without this ability, a manager can't coach employees, build consensus among groups, gain the confidence of customers, or really do anything. And the same is true of parents, coaches, and leaders of all kinds.

There is no leadership without the ability to speak the truth in a unifying manner. Jesus knows this. And so, in today's Gospel reading, he tells us to proclaim his truth without fear. He knows that if we speak the truth – all forms of truth, but especially the truth of his Gospel – his message will spread. Lives will be enriched, families strengthened, businesses improved, governments and organizations purged of corruption, and most importantly, souls will be saved.

Fear not those who can only kill the body. Speak the truth, in all things and about all things, and transform the world.

† 10:28 or, Hell.

‡ 10:29 An *assarion* is a small coin worth one tenth of a drachma or a sixteenth of a denarius. An *assarion* is approximately the wages of one half hour of agricultural labor.

* Catechism of the Catholic Church, Section 41: https://www.vatican.va/archive/ENG0015/__PC.HTM

13th Sunday of Ordinary Time, Sunday 7/2/23

Readings: 2 Kgs 4:8-11, 14-16a, Ps 89:2-3, 16-17, 18-19, Rom 6:3-4, 8-11, Mt 10:37-42
Matthew 10:26—33 World English Bible Catholic Edition

37 He who loves father or mother more than me is not worthy of me; and he who loves son or daughter more than me isn't worthy of me. 38 He who doesn't take his cross and follow after me isn't worthy of me. 39 He who seeks his life will lose it; and he who loses his life for my sake will find it.

40 "He who receives you receives me, and he who receives me receives him who sent me. 41 He who receives a prophet in the name of a prophet will receive a prophet's reward. He who receives a righteous man in the name of a righteous man will receive a righteous man's reward. 42 Whoever gives one of these little ones just a cup of cold water to drink in the name of a disciple, most certainly I tell you, he will in no way lose his reward."

Brothers and sisters, what usually passes for peace is something like a momentary compromise or a negotiated ceasefire between combatants. Open argument stops, but the parties continue to disagree fundamentally. Fighting stops, but beneath the surface there is still anger and hatred. But a truce isn't peace.

There may be periods of time when no rockets pass between Israel and Palestine, but there is no peace.† There are no Chinese troops currently invading Taiwan, and there is no bloodshed at the 38th parallel between North and South Korea at the moment, but there is no peace between these nations. They're not presently killing each other, but there are a great deal of people on both sides who would like to be. That's not peace.

Parents lay down the law and the kids may go along. But behind bedroom doors, there's plenty of grumbling on both sides. Husbands and wives often disagree but bite their tongues and turn a cold shoulder. Discontent continues to simmer. Frustration keeps bubbling. That's not peace either.

Peace only comes when people talk honestly, discuss openly, and solve truly. All of the old tit-for-tat, Hatfield-vs.-McCoy games have to be given up. Truth has to be the highest ideal for all the negotiants. This is why Jesus says that *"He who loves father or mother...son or daughter, more than me isn't worthy of me."* At some point during these discussions, one or both parties must give up on "my country wrong or right."

Each side must forfeit petty grievances, give up on pride, and surrender their avenging will. They must make a sacrifice. A sacrifice. Don't you see? This is why Jesus says, *"He who doesn't take his cross and follow after me isn't worthy of me."* That's how you make peace here and now. And that peace is far greater, an order of magnitude greater, than a mere truce or cease-fire. It's a laudable goal. We should always strive for peace. But there is an even greater Peace – a capital "P" kind of Peace – that's an order of magnitude greater even than that: the Peace of Christ.

The Peace of Christ only inheres when we surrender our lives to Christ. Jesus says, *"He who seeks his life will lose it; and he who loses his life for my sake will find it."* We have let him take control. To find peace between nations and families, we must sacrifice our petty jealousies, indictments, and vendettas. But to find the Peace of Christ we have to sacrifice our whole selves. We have to get beyond the uneasy peace inside our heads and hearts. We must stop rationalizing our lusts, compromising with our sins, holding onto our egos. The Holy Spirit says in Revelation 3:16, *"Because you are lukewarm, and neither hot nor cold, I will vomit you out of my mouth."*

God spits out the half-hearted truce-maker. He spits out those who seek to justify their internal, petty dictators and make deals with the devil. Let's not settle for truces, uneasy peaces, or temporary cease-fires – in the world or in ourselves. Let us seek the true Peace of Christ.

† As I'm editing this volume for publication in January of 2024, my point is further proven to be true. On October 7, 2023 Hamas launched a brutal terrorist attack on Israel which included a coordinated series of bloody massacres. 1,139 were killed – 766 civilians, including 36 children. 3,400 were wounded and 247 civilians were taken captive, of which 132 have still not been freed. 5 people remain missing. These events touched off the Israel-Hamas War, which continues as of this writing. Let us pray that Israel is able to quickly free the remaining hostages, root out all of the terrorists, and that God will bring true peace to the region.

14th Sunday of Ordinary Time, Sunday 7/9/23

Readings: Zec 9:9-10, Ps 145:1-2, 8-9, 10-11, 13-14, Rom 8:9, 11-13, Mt 11:25-30

<u>Matthew 10:26—33 World English Bible Catholic Edition</u>

25 At that time, Jesus answered, "I thank you, Father, Lord of heaven and earth, that you hid these things from the wise and understanding, and revealed them to infants. 26 Yes, Father, for so it was well-pleasing in your sight. 27 All things have been delivered to me by my Father. No one knows the Son, except the Father; neither does anyone know the Father, except the Son and he to whom the Son desires to reveal him.

28 "Come to me, all you who labor and are heavily burdened, and I will give you rest. 29 Take my yoke upon you and learn from me, for I am gentle and humble in heart; and you will find rest for your souls. 30 For my yoke is easy, and my burden is light."

"Come to me all who labor and are heavily burdened and I will give you rest." Brothers and sisters, what kind of labor? Not just any kind of labor. In the Greek this is *kopos*, which is labor to exhaustion, serious toil. And what kind of burden? Well, since Jesus says in the next sentence, "you will find rest for your souls" we can tell that he is talking about soul-crushing burdens – physical and spiritual loads that are too much for one person to bear.

For a year back in 1989 supervised a work crew stacking bricks in a coal-fired brick plant. These men pulled bricks off the kiln cars, still warm from fire. For eight hours a day, five days a week, they stooped, lifted, and stacked. The plant had no air conditioning and in the summer the kilns rose the heat into the triple digits. Sweat pooled in puddles on the deck boards. Nobody got on that platform on purpose, I can assure you of that. Some were ex-cons. Some had dropped out of school. One of my men had declined his previous employer's offer of early retirement at 50% pension, only to be laid off a few months later. At almost 60 years old, uneducated, he found himself stuck on that insufferable platform. All of those men were well aware that they were paying for every last one of their mistakes in a kind of earthly hell. That's the kind of toil Jesus is talking about here.

And Jesus is also talking about spiritual toil. We're talking now about people who have sinned, repented, and made amends, but who still can't give up their crushing guilt. Or people who want to stop bad behaviors, but who can't. Alcoholics, drug and gambling addicts, kleptomaniacs, people stuck in back-breaking spiritual labor with no end in sight.

Jesus begins telling us how to manage these burdens by thanking his Father for revealing the secret to little children. A child, you see, can do nothing alone. A child relies on his or her parents for support. "Daddy, Mommy, tie my shoe." "I feel down and hurt myself." "I'm hungry." Jesus couldn't have carried his cross if it hadn't been for his Father. The Father passes the strength to the Son, and the Son passes it to us. Jesus says, "No one knows the Son, except the Father; neither does anyone know the Father, except the Son and he to whom the Son desires to reveal him."

And then Jesus concludes, "Take my yoke upon you and learn from me, for I am gentle and humble in heart; and you will find rest for your souls. For my yoke is easy, and my burden is light." A yoke is a wooden contraption for tying two oxen together so that they can pull a wagon or a plough. Jesus is telling us that, if we want to find rest for our weary souls, all we have to do is yoke ourselves to him as he is yoked to the Father. He's telling us to rely on him as a child relies on its parents.

It's an easy yoke, and it's not a burden. It is a relief, a fantastic blessing, to know that we don't have to keep shouldering our burdens alone. We can yoke ourselves to the Father, the Son, and the Holy Ghost. This is how we relieve our suffering today and find eternal bliss in the life to come.

15th Sunday of Ordinary Time, Sunday 7/16/23

Readings: Is 55:10-11, Ps 65:10, 11, 12-13, 14, Rom 8:18-23, Mt 13:1-23

<u>Matthew 13:1-23 World English Bible Catholic Edition</u>

On that day Jesus went out of the house and sat by the seaside. 2 Great multitudes gathered to him, so that he entered into a boat and sat; and all the multitude stood on the beach. 3 He spoke to them many things in parables, saying, "Behold, a farmer went out to sow. 4 As he sowed, some seeds fell by the roadside, and the birds came and devoured them. 5 Others fell on rocky ground, where they didn't have much soil, and immediately they sprang up, because they had no depth of earth. 6 When the sun had risen, they were scorched. Because they had no root, they withered away. 7 Others fell among thorns. The thorns grew up and choked them. 8 Others fell on good soil and yielded fruit: some one hundred times as much, some sixty, and some thirty. 9 He who has ears to hear, let him hear."

10 The disciples came, and said to him, "Why do you speak to them in parables?"

*11 He answered them, "To you it is given to know the mysteries
of the Kingdom of Heaven, but it is not given to them. 12
For whoever has, to him will be given, and he will have
abundance; but whoever doesn't have, from him will be taken
away even that which he has. 13 Therefore I speak to them in
parables, because seeing they don't see, and hearing, they don't
hear, neither do they understand. 14 In them the prophecy of
Isaiah is fulfilled, which says,*

'By hearing you will hear,

and will in no way understand;

Seeing you will see,

and will in no way perceive;

15 for this people's heart has grown callous,

their ears are dull of hearing,

and they have closed their eyes;

or else perhaps they might perceive with their eyes,

hear with their ears,

understand with their heart,

and would turn again,

*and I would heal them.'**

*16 "But blessed are your eyes, for they see; and your ears, for
they hear. 17 For most certainly I tell you that many prophets*

and righteous men desired to see the things which you see, and didn't see them; and to hear the things which you hear, and didn't hear them.

18 "Hear, then, the parable of the farmer. 19 When anyone hears the word of the Kingdom and doesn't understand it, the evil one comes and snatches away that which has been sown in his heart. This is what was sown by the roadside. 20 What was sown on the rocky places, this is he who hears the word and immediately with joy receives it; 21 yet he has no root in himself, but endures for a while. When oppression or persecution arises because of the word, immediately he stumbles. 22 What was sown among the thorns, this is he who hears the word, but the cares of this age and the deceitfulness of riches choke the word, and he becomes unfruitful. 23 What was sown on the good ground, this is he who hears the word and understands it, who most certainly bears fruit and produces, some one hundred times as much, some sixty, and some thirty."

In traditional Karate, the only acceptable color for a uniform is white. White signifies a blank sheet of paper. It says that everyone is prepared – students and instructors alike – to watch and listen, to learn lessons, and to take notes. In a similar vein, the Greek philosopher Socrates said that wonder is the beginning of wisdom. He believed and taught that the truth emerged out of sincere dialogue – asking genuine questions and giving honest answers.

This is universal wisdom. If we approach a situation, problem, person, or social encounter – literally anything – with a sense of wonder, curiosity, and receptivity, we will learn things. We find this wisdom offered up by many wise teachers and philosophers across the globe. But what we are seeing in today's Gospel reading a much deeper exploration of this dense philosophical concept.

He explains that some, when they receive the truth, are not curious at all. They have no wonder, no receptivity. They shrug it off. This is the seed the evil one snatches away. Others are moved emotionally and are inspired for a time. But they don't ground what they've learned in their heart and in their actions. As soon as things get difficult, because of peer pressure, persecution, or the temptations of riches and social status, they give up.

When asked why he teaches in parables, Jesus says, *"To you it is given to know the mysteries of the Kingdom of Heaven, but it is not given to them."* He's saying, "I'm giving it you straight because you get it, but I'm not giving it to them. They get parables." And then he adds, *"For whoever has, to him will be given, and he will have abundance; but whoever doesn't have, from him will be taken away even that which he has."* Here he expounds the universal wisdom that those who have wonder, curiosity, and receptivity will be drawn ever forward into greater and greater understanding. But he adds a unique observation: those who don't cultivate wonder, curiosity, and receptivity will stagnate.

Nothing stays the same.

A scientist who wants to stay relevant and keep innovating must stay up-to-date. Many professions, like lawyers, doctors and accountants, are required to engage in continuing education in order to be licensed. This wisdom is everywhere. But Jesus' singular observation is deeper still. The same is true of spiritual knowledge. If we rest on our laurels, and feel that we've made our successes, done our good deeds, and had all our great insights, we begin to fall into an "I have arrived" standpoint, or a "been there, done that" outlook regarding the work of the spirit. What little wisdom we've stored up will depreciate, perhaps even all the way down to hell.

Jesus' solution to the hardness of some human hearts, to the lack of wonder and curiosity, is to teach in parables. The Hebrew word for a parable is *mashal* which means "riddle." A riddle begs to be answered. It's as natural as breathing! Jesus' parables have that quality. They are like seeds. If we are fertile ground, if his word is watered with wonder, warmed by the sun of curiosity, and tended with receptivity, his teaching will grow into ever deeper understanding, even unto the Kingdom of Heaven, to salvation in Christ Jesus.

* 13:15 Isaiah 6:9-10

16ᵗʰ Sunday of Ordinary Time, Sunday 7/23/23

Readings: Wis 12:13, 16-19, Ps 86:5-6, 9-10, 15-16, Rom 8:26-27, Mt 13:24-43

<u>Matthew 13:24-43 World English Bible, Catholic Edition</u>

24 He set another parable before them, saying, "The Kingdom of Heaven is like a man who sowed good seed in his field, 25 but while people slept, his enemy came and sowed darnel weeds† also among the wheat, and went away. 26 But when the blade sprang up and produced grain, then the darnel weeds appeared also. 27 The servants of the householder came and said to him, 'Sir, didn't you sow good seed in your field? Where did these darnel weeds come from?'

28 "He said to them, 'An enemy has done this.'

"The servants asked him, 'Do you want us to go and gather them up?'

29 "But he said, 'No, lest perhaps while you gather up the darnel weeds, you root up the wheat with them. 30 Let both grow together until the harvest, and in the harvest time I will tell the reapers, "First, gather up the darnel weeds, and bind them in bundles to burn them; but gather the wheat into my barn."' "

31 *He set another parable before them, saying, "The Kingdom of Heaven is like a grain of mustard seed which a man took, and sowed in his field, 32 which indeed is smaller than all seeds. But when it is grown, it is greater than the herbs and becomes a tree, so that the birds of the air come and lodge in its branches."*

33 *He spoke another parable to them. "The Kingdom of Heaven is like yeast which a woman took and hid in three measures‡ of meal, until it was all leavened."*

34 *Jesus spoke all these things in parables to the multitudes; and without a parable, he didn't speak to them, 35 that it might be fulfilled which was spoken through the prophet, saying,*

"I will open my mouth in parables;

*I will utter things hidden from the foundation of the world."**

36 *Then Jesus sent the multitudes away, and went into the house. His disciples came to him, saying, "Explain to us the parable of the darnel weeds of the field."*

37 *He answered them, "He who sows the good seed is the Son of Man, 38 the field is the world, the good seeds are the children of the Kingdom, and the darnel weeds are the children of the evil one. 39 The enemy who sowed them is the devil. The harvest is the end of the age, and the reapers are angels. 40 As therefore the darnel weeds are gathered up and burned with fire; so will it be at the end of this age. 41 The Son of Man will send out his angels, and they will gather out of his Kingdom all things that cause stumbling and those who do iniquity, 42 and will cast them into the furnace of fire. There will be weeping and*

gnashing of teeth. 43 Then the righteous will shine like the sun in the Kingdom of their Father. He who has ears to hear, let him hear."

Various translations use different words for "weed" in Matthew 13:25. The King James says "tares" were sowed among the wheat. Tare is an old-fashioned word for a weed. The Douay Rheims uses "cockles" and the RSV just says "weeds." But, interestingly, the Greek and Latin both use the word *zizanium* which is a weed that closely resembles wheat. I believe the meaning here is that there are Christians, and there are look-alike Christians, and it's hard to tell the difference. But Jesus knows. And when he returns to judge the quick and dead, he's going to separate the two. There's going to be a reckoning.

As I meditated on this scripture, I remembered a man I haven't seen in many years. When my father passed away in 2008, my mother and I were stumbling through the darkness of grief. Thankfully, my father had prepaid for everything and made all of the arrangements. The only major thing we had to do was arrange the funeral service itself. The funeral director put me in touch with a total stranger named Reverend Harry Bowman.[1] Reverend Bowman was a whip thin man in his 60s who had officiated hundreds of funerals. He met with us to prepare the eulogy and service, Mom first, then me. When it was my turn, he gently asked me questions about my father, and got me talking. I felt like I'd known Reverend Bowman my whole life. I told him all about my father, about how he was a god-fearing man who had considered becoming a Presbyterian minister in his youth, and who read the Bible to me from the time I was born until middle school.

During the interview he asked me why we weren't church-going. I explained that some kind of financial scandal involving the minister and the board had disillusioned my mother and father. They had left the church for good. As for me, I said, I just grew up and stopped believing. I'm ashamed to say that I asked him, "You don't actually believe all that stuff, like Jesus rising from the grave, do you?"

He smiled warmly. And with calm confidence, he said, "Yes, yes indeed. Without question. And you should too." I confess, I remember that he did a good job with the service, but I really don't remember the rest of our conversation or even the details of the service. It has all been swallowed up in the hazy clouds of grief and time. I do remember many people telling me how lovely Reverend Bowman's eulogy was. But his witness to the Resurrection of Jesus Christ echoes down the years. And by the way, he also helped me bury my mother, eulogizing her when she passed in 2016.

In my story, the weeds that look like wheat are the ones whose betrayal of their church so disillusioned my parents – and who knows how many others! – that they left and never went back. Woe to those look-alike weeds brothers and sisters! Jesus said, "The Son of Man will send out his angels, and they will gather out of his Kingdom all things that cause stumbling and those who do iniquity, and will cast them into the furnace of fire."

And the good seed? Well that's Reverend Harry Bowman, who stood firm in his witness to the truth of the Resurrection. Who patiently, calmly spoke the truth to a confused man like me. Who has made a career out of guiding strangers through their darkest hours, steering them patiently toward Christ.

† 13:25 darnel is a weed grass (probably bearded darnel or lolium temulentum) that looks very much like wheat until it is mature, when the difference becomes very apparent.

‡ 13:33 literally, three *sata*. Three *sata* is about 39 liters or a bit more than a bushel

* 13:35 Psalm 78:2

[1] Shortly after writing this homily I send a thank you letter to Rev. Bowman and we exchanged correspondence. He was as gracious as ever. This book is dedicated to his patience, grace, and witness.

17th Sunday of Ordinary Time, Sunday 7/30/23

Readings: 1 Kgs 3:5, 7-12, Ps 119:57, 72, 76-77, 127-128, 129-130, Rom 8:28-30, Mt 13:44-52

<u>Matthew 13:44-52 World English Bible, Catholic Edition</u>

Jesus said to his disciples:

"Again, the Kingdom of Heaven is like treasure hidden in the field, which a man found and hid. In his joy, he goes and sells all that he has and buys that field.

45 "Again, the Kingdom of Heaven is like a man who is a merchant seeking fine pearls, 46 who having found one pearl of great price, he went and sold all that he had and bought it.

47 "Again, the Kingdom of Heaven is like a dragnet that was cast into the sea and gathered some fish of every kind, 48 which, when it was filled, fishermen drew up on the beach. They sat down and gathered the good into containers, but the bad they threw away. 49 So it will be in the end of the world.§ The angels will come and separate the wicked from among the righteous, 50 and will cast them into the furnace of fire. There will be weeping and gnashing of teeth." 51 Jesus said to them, "Have you understood all these things?"

They answered him, "Yes, Lord."

52 He said to them, "Therefore every scribe who has been made a disciple in the Kingdom of Heaven is like a man who is a householder, who brings out of his treasure new and old things."

When I was kid, my father would let me borrow the car. He didn't ask much, only that when I returned it to the driveway, its interior be as neat as I found it, and that the gas tank be filled up. Well, thank goodness he was an infinitely patient and forgiving man because, like a lot of teens, I didn't follow the rules. So he stopped letting me borrow his nice car. I had to drive the battered old station wagon that he used for his contracting business.

I still didn't learn my lesson, I'm sorry to say. I drove it too fast and wrecked it. At that point there was only one thing he could do: sell me a car. My mother needed a new car, so he agreed to sell me her old 1970 Pinto for $200. That was a lot of money in 1978, especially if you're a 17-year-old bagging groceries. Now, let me tell you, that car I took care of. I drove that thing for almost ten years – I even brought my first child home from the hospital in that thing!

Lesson learned.

And that's the lesson Jesus wants us to learn. *"The Kingdom of Heaven is like treasure hidden in the field, which a man found and hid. In his joy, he goes and sells all that he has and buys that field."* The man in this story doesn't own the field. He can't possibly treat the treasure the way someone does who's invested in it, who has taken ownership of its perfection, its power, and its perpetuation. Jesus wants us to buy into his wisdom – even more than I bought into that old Pinto.

Jesus says, *"the Kingdom of Heaven is like a man...who having found one pearl of great price, he went and sold all that he had and bought it."* Jesus wants to sell all we have to take ownership of his Kingdom.

What do we sell? We sell our pride for humility in Christ. We sell our greed and our envy for the spirit of sharing. We sell our wrath for patience and our gluttony for food to feed the hungry. We sell our lust for attention to shower on our spouses. And we trade our sloth for the energy to work on behalf of our neighbors and our churches.

Jesus says, *"Therefore every scribe who has been made a disciple in the Kingdom of Heaven is like a man who is a householder, who brings out of his treasure new and old things."* Jewish scribes copied Torah scrolls and were extremely careful and accurate experts in the law and the prophets. They were consulted for answers to serious legal and ethical questions. And when a householder digs into his savings, when he pulls out some of his treasure, it is only for something of paramount importance. If we're smart, we don't touch our treasure troves – our retirement plans, our IRAs, and our 401Ks – unless it's absolutely essential. If we squander it, we'll have no way to take care ourselves in our old age.

Those of us who quote the Bible, who offer up its laws and prophecies to this culture, are being told to treat what we are dealing with in the same way as the householder treats his treasure – as if the salvation of ourselves, our families, our neighbors, and all souls on earth, depends on it.

Because it does.

§ 13:49 or, end of the age.

The Transfiguration of the Lord, Sunday 8/6/23

Readings: Dn 7:9-10, 13-14, Ps 97:1-2, 5-6, 9, 2 Pt 1:16-19, Mt 17:1-9

<u>Daniel 7:9-10, 13-14 World English Bible Catholic Edition</u>

9 "I watched until thrones were placed,

and one who was ancient of days sat.

His clothing was white as snow,

and the hair of his head like pure wool.

His throne was fiery flames,

and its wheels burning fire.

10 A fiery stream issued and came out from before him.

Thousands of thousands ministered to him.

Ten thousand times ten thousand stood before him.

The judgment was set.

The books were opened.

13 "I saw in the night visions, and behold, one like a son of man came with the clouds, and he came to the ancient of days, and they brought him near before him. 14 Dominion was given him, with glory and a kingdom, that all the peoples, nations, and languages should serve him. His dominion is an everlasting dominion, which will not pass away, and his kingdom will not be destroyed.

Today's reading from Daniel is abbreviated so as to highlight, in a simple and direct way, an Old Testament prophecy of the

Transfiguration which we celebrate today. But if we examine the whole of Daniel 7, we can get an even deeper understanding of what the Transfiguration is finally all about.

The verses just before today's describe Daniel's vision of four beasts emerging from the sea. The first three bear some resemblance to familiar animals. But the fourth creature, which is "awesome and powerful, and exceedingly strong," defies imagination, and we're given some bizarre details regarding its horns.

8 "I considered the horns, and behold, another horn came up among them, a little one, before which three of the first horns were plucked up by the roots: and behold, in this horn were eyes like the eyes of a man, and a mouth speaking great [boastful] *things.*

What on earth can this nightmarish image mean? Ten is the perfect number, the basis of math and the number of the Decalogue, the Ten Commandments. Ten is God's law. A terrifying, talking horn with eyes and mouth appears in the midst of the ten horns, and drives out three of them. Out of ten (God's law), three are driven (the Holy Trinity). Now, with this new horn added, there are eight. The eight-pointed star is the symbol of the Babylonian goddess Inanna. The city of Babylon had eight gates. In Revelation, the antichrist is the eighth king. Eight is chaos.

The sacred *shofar*, the Jewish horn, is blown on High Holy Days. *Shofar* is Hebrew for "listen." The shofar proclaims to the people, "Listen to God!" and to God it proclaims, "God, your people are listening!" But the evil horn on the fourth beast from Daniel's nightmare is the opposite. It is one of the most disturbing symbols in the Bible. In Daniel 7:25 we read that the talking horn "wi*ll speak words against the Most High, and will wear out the saints of the Most High. He will plan to change the times and the law.'"* Rather than proclaiming God's truth, this horn speaks for itself. It literally toots its own horn and proclaims its own truth, turning the law into chaos.

God help us, but this nightmarish horn that proclaims its own truths is sounding everywhere right now. Voices of chaos are booming – out of our televisions, on social media, on billboards, howling from the mouths of performers, politicians, and pundits, tooting and honking, undermining God truth. They are loud today, but were even louder and deadlier in the days of Peter, James and John. James would be the first martyred, followed by Peter. And it's in that context that Jesus takes theses three apostles to a high place and gives them a glimpse of his power and glory, to give them heart. To carry them through the trials and tribulations he knew they would face.

The Transfiguration which we celebrate today – Jesus appearing with his face shining like the sun and his garments as white as the light – is a foretaste of the glory to come. Do not be disheartened in the face of oppressors. Do not be worn down and led astray by voices seeking to subvert the rituals and laws that are the foundation of our society and our religion.

As Daniel's vision predicts, and the Transfiguration prefigures, God's *dominion is an everlasting dominion, which will not pass away, and his kingdom will not be destroyed.* The voices of evil and dissention will be silenced. God will reign forever and ever.

19th Sunday of Ordinary Time, Sunday 8/13/23

Readings: 1 Kgs 19:9a, 11-13a, Ps 85:9, 10, 11-12, 13-14, Rom 9:1-5, Mt 14:22-33

<u>1 Kgs 19:9a, 11-13a World English Bible Catholic Edition</u>

He [Elijah] came to a cave there [Mt. Horeb], and camped there.

11 The Lord said to him, "Go out and stand on the mountain before the LORD."

Behold, the LORD passed by, and a great and strong wind tore the mountains and broke in pieces the rocks before the LORD; but the LORD was not in the wind. After the wind there was an earthquake; but the LORD was not in the earthquake. 12 After the earthquake a fire passed; but the LORD was not in the fire. After the fire, there was a still small voice. 13 When Elijah heard it, he wrapped his face in his mantle, went out, and stood in the entrance of the cave.

Matthew 14:22-33 World English Bible Catholic Edition

22 Immediately Jesus made the disciples get into the boat and go ahead of him to the other side, while he sent the multitudes away. 23 After he had sent the multitudes away, he went up *into the mountain by himself to pray. When evening had come, he was there alone. 24 But the boat was now in the middle of the sea, distressed by the waves, for the wind was contrary. 25 In the fourth watch of the night,† Jesus came to them, walking on the sea.* 26 When the disciples saw him walking on the sea, they were troubled, saying, "It's a ghost!" and they cried out for fear. 27 But immediately Jesus spoke to them, saying, "Cheer up! It is I! ‡ Don't be afraid."*

28 Peter answered him and said, "Lord, if it is you, command me to come to you on the waters."

29 He said, "Come!"

Peter stepped down from the boat and walked on the waters to come to Jesus. 30 But when he saw that the wind was strong, he was afraid, and beginning to sink, he cried out, saying, "Lord, save me!"

31 Immediately Jesus stretched out his hand, took hold of him, and said to him, "You of little faith, why did you doubt?" 32 When they got up into the boat, the wind ceased. 33 Those who were in the boat came and worshiped him, saying, "You are truly the Son of God!"

At the mountain of God, Elijah is exposed to the remarkable power of nature – thunder, lightning, wind, landslides, and fire. But God is not in these things. With his voice God spoke nature into existence. And so it is God's whisper that causes Elija to cover his face in humility, wonder, and awe, not the storm.

The pagan nature-worshippers in the countries that surrounded God's people on every side at that time – the Greeks and the Romans, the Egyptians and the Babylonians, and all the rest –had their storm gods. They had their Zeus, their Set, their Marduk and their Ba'al. God's creation is incredible, it's beautiful, amazing, awe inspiring, worthy of love, care, and respect and all of that. But it's not worthy of worship. Nature and its fury are not God. But those pagans, if they had been in Elijah's place, would've bowed down and worshipped the storm. They would've been unable to hear God's whisper over all the racket.

But Elijah is fearless and he is listening. God tells him to leave the safety of the cave and go out into the storm. Does Elijah cower in fear? No. Can you imagine? What faith! What courage! And then, what does he hear? What is his reward? God's faintest whisper. And that's enough for any person who loves God.

In Romans 9:1-5 St. Paul says that he would sacrifice himself and cut himself off from Christ if it meant that this people would hear God's whisper and come toward the voice of Christ. He says, "look, you've got the law, the covenants, the worship, the prophets and the patriarchs, but you're distracted by the flash and flare. What you need to do is hear and follow the Word."

Peter is literally in the same boat as the Israelites to whom St. Paul is speaking. Peter wants to join Jesus on top the water – to stand above nature, to be above all of the old pagan ideas. Peter wants to have the courage and faith of Elijah. But the scripture says, *"Peter stepped down from the boat and walked on the waters to come to Jesus. But when he saw that the wind was strong, he was afraid, and beginning to sink, he cried out, saying, "Lord, save me!"* Jesus pulls him up. Back in the boat, the storm passes. Then, of course, Peter and the other apostles say, *"You are truly the Son of God!"* Brothers and sisters, it sure is a lot easier to hear God's truth when life isn't stormy, isn't it?

That's the boat we're in today. We're surrounded by nature worshippers who bow down before the power of climate change; by the idolatry of money, lust, fame, and power. Everywhere we look are those who are fearful of political earthquakes and terrified by the fires of social unrest. We're hemmed in on all sides by folks who aren't even trying to listen for God's awesome whisper.

If you're fearful, that's okay. Pray to Jesus Christ as Peter did. He'll extend his hand and keep you from drowning. And above all, listen for Christ's Word amidst the storm and take heart. Through Christ, *"Kindness and truth shall meet; justice and peace shall kiss. Truth shall spring out of the earth, and justice shall look down from heaven."* (Psalm 85:10-11) Through Christ, all things are possible (Matthew 19:26).

† 14:25 The night was equally divided into four watches, so the fourth watch is approximately 3:00 a.m. to sunrise.

* 14:25 See Job 9:8

‡ 14:27 or, I AM!

20th Sunday of Ordinary Time, Sunday 8/20/23

Readings: Is 56:1, 6-7, Ps 67:2-3, 5, 6, 8, Rom 11:13-15, 29-32, Mt 15:21-28

<u>Matthew 15:21-28 World English Bible Catholic Edition</u>

Jesus went out from there and withdrew into the region of Tyre and Sidon. 22 Behold, a Canaanite woman came out from those borders and cried, saying, "Have mercy on me, Lord, you son of David! My daughter is severely possessed by a demon!"

23 But he answered her not a word.

His disciples came and begged him, saying, "Send her away; for she cries after us."

24 But he answered, "I wasn't sent to anyone but the lost sheep of the house of Israel."

25 But she came and worshiped him, saying, "Lord, help me."

26 But he answered, "It is not appropriate to take the children's bread and throw it to the dogs."

27 But she said, "Yes, Lord, but even the dogs eat the crumbs which fall from their masters' table."

*28 Then Jesus answered her, "Woman, great is your faith! Be it
done to you even as you desire." And her daughter was healed
from that hour.*

Imagine you are attending a child's football practice. Some distance
away there is a kid watching who's been following the team around for
days. And the players say, "Coach, get rid of that kid will you? He's
driving us nuts." But the coach wants to see if the kid has what it takes
be a player. So the coach says to the kid, "I'm not your coach kid. I'm
here to coach these players and these players only. You got that?"

Now, some youngsters would give up. But not this one. He decides
to show the coach what he's made of. He starts following the coach's
instructions and copying the team drills. He starts to really sweat and
work. The coach notices. He comes over and he says, "Look kid, my
players have earned their jerseys. I don't disrespect the team by giving a
jersey to every loser punk who follows the team around."

Many kids would be insulted. But not this one, he's too humble
for that. He knows he sort of stinks and that he needs a good coach
to realize his potential. And many kids would get discouraged and give
up. But not him – he doesn't need easy, he just needs possible. So
he tells the coach, "Water boys and mascots get jerseys though, don't
they?" Not only is he humble, but he's also plucky and smart.

Now the coach knows all he needs to know. He says, "Okay kid,
you win. You're on the team."

This is a secular version of the story in today's gospel reading.
Traveling in the region of Tyre and Sidon, Jesus is pursued by a woman
whose daughter has been possessed by a demon. Jesus ignores her
completely at first. But she follows him so long, and so relentlessly, that
eventually the disciples ask Jesus to send her away. But Jesus doesn't.
Instead he says to her, "*I wasn't sent to anyone but the lost sheep of the
house of Israel.*"

Although his mission is first to the Hebrews, Jesus has come to all the people of the world. Is Jesus lying to her here? No, Jesus doesn't lie. Jesus is like the football coach who told the kid, "I'm not your coach kid. I'm here to coach these players and these players only."

This is a challenge.

And the Canaanite woman accepts the challenge. She worships Jesus saying, "Lord, help me." She demonstrates to Jesus, just like the kid doing drills on the sidelines, that she's not just hanging around. She came to work.

To this Jesus answers, "It is not appropriate to take the children's bread and throw it to the dogs." And just like the kid, she isn't insulted. She is humble, smart, and plucky too. She doesn't need easy, she just needs possible. She says, "Yes, Lord, but even the dogs eat the crumbs which fall from their masters' table."

At last Jesus has heard all he needs to hear. He says, "Woman, great is your faith! Be it done to you even as you desire." And her daughter is healed.

Brothers and sisters, millions of people every day send up prayers that aren't answered. Why is God silent? We can't always answer that. His ways are not our ways (Isaiah 55:8-9). But at least some of the time, it's to encourage us to work harder. God wants us to be like the Canaanite woman. He wants us to be like the kid on the sidelines who desperately wants to learn from the coach and be on the team. He wants us to demonstrate our faith, to be strong, and to be persistent in our prayers.

And he wants us to never, ever give up.

21st Sunday of Ordinary Time, Sunday 8/27/23

Readings: Is 22:19-23, Ps 138:1-2, 2-3, 6, 8, Rom 11:33-36, Mt 16:13-20

<u>Matthew 16:13-20 World English Bible Catholic Edition</u>

Now when Jesus came into the parts of Caesarea Philippi, he asked his disciples, saying, "Who do men say that I, the Son of Man, am?"

14 They said, "Some say John the Baptizer, some, Elijah, and others, Jeremiah or one of the prophets."

15 He said to them, "But who do you say that I am?"

16 Simon Peter answered, "You are the Christ, the Son of the living God."

17 Jesus answered him, "Blessed are you, Simon Bar Jonah, for flesh and blood has not revealed this to you, but my Father who is in heaven. 18 I also tell you that you are Peter,† and on this rock ‡ I will build my assembly, and the gates of Hades§ will not prevail against it. 19 I will give to you the keys of the Kingdom of Heaven, and whatever you bind on earth will have been bound in heaven; and whatever you release on earth will have been released in heaven." 20 Then he commanded the disciples that they should tell no one that he was Jesus the Christ.

In today's Gospel reading, God puts a frail and faulty mere mortal in charge of his precious church, placing the mystical Body of Christ on Earth into the hands of a fisherman from Bethsaida (John 1:44). Obviously he was a successful leader. If he hadn't been, we would not be gathered together today to celebrate the Eucharist. The church would've been snuffed out. How is it possible for an imperfect fisherman, so human that he denied Jesus three times, to be successful? Is this a miracle?

As a martial arts coach, corporate manager, mentor, and priest, I have three decades of experience raising people up from inexperience to management, from awkward and fearful to coordinated and courageous, and from doubtful to faithful. This process is always and everywhere the same. It amounts to convincing the person to accept their potential and to allow themselves to become something new.

In 1990 my martial arts coach asked if I wanted a position teaching martial arts to inner city kids twice per week. I took the job. And I quickly learned that if you don't quit, and if you engage with the process with dedication and sincerity, a miracle takes place. Kids and adults ask you questions. You have to listen intently and answer sincerely. Every appropriate answer requires you to think, to work, to do research, and to properly order your thoughts. A good teacher learns at the same rate as his students. As a knife is sharpened on a whetstone, the stone is also smoothed. In a good school, there is a conversation. When I got my first management job, I discovered that the same truth manifested itself in the business world. In a strong business, there is a dialogue between management and staff, between managers, and between employees.

In every organization where this approach is taken – educational, commercial, religious, or what-have-you – everyone is elevated together. Out of this dialogue, truth and excellence emerge.

There is no doubt in my mind that this is what happened to Peter. He engaged with his new position as the rock of the church. He discovered that if he fostered a healthy dialogue – if he really listened to his flock and allowed himself to grow through answering their toughest questions with patience and careful preparation – everyone improved. He got stronger and more effective. And so did they.

Is this miraculous? Or is this just common-sense management and good old-fashioned patience and hard work?

In John 1 we read "In the beginning was the Word, and the Word was with God, and the Word was God." In the Greek, the Word is *Logos*. *Logos* is the root of the Greek *diálogos* and the English word *dialogue*. When we have honest and patient dialogues – when we speak and listen with sincerity as Jesus did – the truth emerges from these conversations. Problems are solved, difficulties are overcome, people get stronger and more capable, and the world is lifted up.

This is extremely profound. Whoever has ears, let him hear: If the universe was meaningless – if there was no God, no Son, no Word, no Holy Ghost – there would be no intelligibility at all. All that would emerge from conversations would be pure chaos. There would only be more fighting, more failure, more fractionation. But that's not how it is at all. Because God's order sustains all of creation, the truth is discoverable and goodness is emergent from interactions undertaken in the spirit of love.

So yes, brothers and sisters, it is a profound miracle and proof God's Logos that a poor Jewish fisherman was able to be the rock of the church. And it is an equal miracle when each of us allows ourselves to be the rocks of our families, our businesses, our communities and our nations.

† 16:18 Peter's name, Petros in Greek, is the word for a specific rock or stone.

‡ 16:18 Greek, *petra*, a rock mass or bedrock.

§ 16:18 or, Hell

22nd Sunday of Ordinary Time, Sunday 9/3/23

Readings: Jer 20:7-9, Ps 63:2, 3-4, 5-6, 8-9, Rom 12:1-2, Mt 16:21-27

<u>Matthew 16:21-27 World English Bible Catholic Edition</u>

From that time, Jesus began to show his disciples that he must go to Jerusalem and suffer many things from the elders, chief priests, and scribes, and be killed, and the third day be raised up.

22 Peter took him aside and began to rebuke him, saying, "Far be it from you, Lord! This will never be done to you."

23 But he turned and said to Peter, "Get behind me, Satan! You are a stumbling block to me, for you are not setting your mind on the things of God, but on the things of men."

24 Then Jesus said to his disciples, "If anyone desires to come after me, let him deny himself, take up his cross, and follow me. 25 For whoever desires to save his life will lose it, and whoever will lose his life for my sake will find it. 26 For what will it profit a man if he gains the whole world and forfeits his life? Or what will a man give in exchange for his life? 27 For the Son of Man will come in the glory of his Father with his angels, and then he will render to everyone according to his deeds. 28 Most certainly I tell you, there are some standing here who will in no way taste of death until they see the Son of Man coming in his Kingdom."

Today we read, *"Get behind me, Satan! You are a stumbling block to me, for you are not setting your mind on the things of God, but on the things of men"* or in other popular translations, *"you are thinking not as God does, but as humans do."* (Mt 16:23). How can we be expected to think the way that the Creator of the Universe does? Is this even possible for us?

We might instinctively feel as though Jesus' expectations, voiced first to Peter and then extended to all of his disciples in the next sentence, are unfairly high. But there is one very important fact to consider: God became man and walked among us, showing us the way to walk in the world. Jesus rose from the dead and promised us a share in his Resurrection in the world to come. We know the reality of the expectations and the reward.

But at the point when Jesus said the words we read today, Peter and the other disciples had only promises, not proof. Practical, common-sense people like them – people like many of us! – are solution-oriented. We tend to think positively and to assume that every bad situation can be fixed, and every known obstacle can be avoided. Peter thinks surely there is a way to prevent Jesus from having to suffer and die! We tend to be like Peter. If we know there's a traffic jam, we can choose another route. If we know a hurricane is coming, we can board up the windows and head to safer ground.

But common-sense thinking like this, when it comes to morality, is just as much a stumbling block to us as it was to Peter. In this life we face many practical choices large and small. Will we compromise our beliefs or hold fast? Will we say grace at the restaurant or stay silent to fit in? Hide the mechanical problems with our car so that we can sell it to some sucker for a better price? Ignore the Commandments when they're inconvenient or costly? Will we justify shopping on Sunday by saying it provides income for the poor, disrespect our parents because they deserve it for being annoying, or steal from a rich man because he has plenty?

Jesus did what he did and said what he said, come what may. We must do likewise. The Greek word for "stumbling block" is *skandalos*, the bait stick that triggers an animal trap. Let us not be snared. The path of expediency runs along the edge of a lake of fire and, as the saying goes, "The road to hell is paved with good intentions."

23rd Sunday of Ordinary Time, Sunday 9/10/23

Readings: Ez 33:7-9, Ps 95:1-2, 6-7, 8-9, Rom 13:8-10, Mt 18:15-20

<u>Matthew 18:15-20 World English Bible Catholic Edition</u>

Jesus said,

"If your brother sins against you, go, show him his fault between you and him alone. If he listens to you, you have gained back your brother. 16 But if he doesn't listen, take one or two more with you, that at the mouth of two or three witnesses every word may be established. 17 If he refuses to listen to them, tell it to the assembly. If he refuses to hear the assembly also, let him be to you as a Gentile or a tax collector. 18 Most certainly I tell you, whatever things you bind on earth will have been bound in heaven, and whatever things you release on earth will have been released in heaven. 19 Again, assuredly I tell you, that if two of you will agree on earth concerning anything that they will ask, it will be done for them by my Father who is in heaven. 20 For where two or three are gathered together in my name, there I am in the middle of them."*

The modern way of seeing is the materialist-rationalist view. Only those things which can be measured, quantified, and studied are real. All of modernity has been and continues to be a long, complex, and lurid celebration of the sin of idolatry. Material realities are elevated to highest standing, and the things that are sacred – God, love, beauty, truth, justice – are deemed fluid, immaterial, unimportant, or dangerous. This is why, during the height of the COVID pandemic panic, science was worshipped as ultimate truth while our churches were deemed "non-essential services" and ordered closed, despite having been hospitals serving the physically, spiritually, and mentally ill.

The faulty and idolatrous modern way of seeing was perhaps first succinctly described by Plato in his allegory of the cave in the 4th century BC. Plato describes people who, for their entire lives, have been chained in a cave facing a wall. All they can see are the shadows that are cast against the wall as other individuals go about their daily activities. As far as the people chained in the cave are aware, the shadows are real. Not knowing any better, their "reality" is a world of shadow puppets. Only when they are unchained can they see the actual forms, the real truths that cast the shadows.

The early fathers of the Christian church saw Plato's cave as a wise pagan precursor to their view that ideas are more "real" than objects. Christians know, for example, that all kings and leaders are destined to imperfection because they are shadows of the Heavenly King. Saul, David, Solomon, and Pharoah are all different people, but they are all the same in the sense that they are pale shadows of our King in Heaven. Heaven contains the realm of ideas, and it casts long shadows into our daily lives.

To the ancient mind – and this is very, very hard for modern people to step into – *physical examples are less real than the ideas they exemplify.* We need to get into this mindset in order to fully understand today's Gospel reading: the idea is more real than the material. This is because the material world itself is based on an idea – an idea in the mind of God! – which he spoke into existence.

The only true bridge between the realm of ideas – Heaven – and the realm of the material is Jesus Christ. He is the Word made Flesh – the ideal become real. He is the perfect King alive. And this is why, in today's reading, Jesus says that they only way to properly adjudicate a dispute is to gather together in his name, which is to say, in a manner that places Jesus Christ in the center of our assembly. Only if we do that can we have any hope of permitting on earth what is permitted in heaven, and forbidding on earth what is forbidden in heaven.

Every conflict has its details and particularities. In a sense that they are all different. But it's truer still to see, as the ancients did, that all disagreements are the same insofar as they cannot be properly solved unless we invite Jesus Christ, the Prince of Peace, to be in our midst.

*18:16 Deuteronomy 19:15

24th Sunday of Ordinary Time, Sunday 9/17/23

Readings: Sir 27:30—28:7, Ps 103:1-2, 3-4, 9-10, 11-12, Rom 14:7-9, Mt 18:21-35

<u>Matthew 18:21-35 World English Bible Catholic Edition</u>

21 Then Peter came and said to him, "Lord, how often shall my brother sin against me, and I forgive him? Until seven times?"

22 Jesus said to him, "I don't tell you until seven times, but, until seventy times seven. 23 Therefore the Kingdom of Heaven is like a certain king who wanted to settle accounts with his servants. 24 When he had begun to settle, one was brought to him who owed him ten thousand talents.§ 25 But because he couldn't pay, his lord commanded him to be sold, with his wife, his children, and all that he had, and payment to be made. 26 The servant therefore fell down and knelt before him, saying, 'Lord, have patience with me, and I will repay you all!' 27 The lord of that servant, being moved with compassion, released him and forgave him the debt.

28 "But that servant went out and found one of his fellow servants who owed him one hundred denarii,† and he grabbed him and took him by the throat, saying, 'Pay me what you owe!'

29 "So his fellow servant fell down at his feet and begged him, saying, 'Have patience with me, and I will repay you!' 30 He would not, but went and cast him into prison until he should pay back that which was due. 31 So when his fellow servants saw what was done, they were exceedingly sorry, and came and told their lord all that was done. 32 Then his lord called him in and said to him, 'You wicked servant! I forgave you all that debt because you begged me. 33 Shouldn't you also have had mercy on your fellow servant, even as I had mercy on you?' 34 His lord was angry, and delivered him to the tormentors until he should pay all that was due to him. 35 So my heavenly Father will also do to you, if you don't each forgive your brother from your hearts for his misdeeds."

When children squabble and fight, every caregiver with a grain of common sense brings the children together to apologize and grant forgiveness. Every supervisor at every company has at some point brought together quarrelling employees and done the very same thing. Why is the importance of forgiveness so obvious, and yet, so often avoided?

We could try to argue that we grasp the wisdom of forgiveness because we've seen brutal, ever-escalating, revenge wars play themselves out between criminal gangs and crime syndicates. Or because we've seen families wrecked by never-ending feuds and arguments, and teen lives wrecked by situations where a slight leads to a slap, a slap leads to a stab, and a stab leads to a drive-by shooting. But that would be a faulty argument. The sensibility of forgiveness is logical, but it isn't conscious. When we decide whether or not to forgive, we don't think through the entire history of sociology, and go read Martin Buber's great book on morality <u>I and Thou</u> before we take action. Forgiveness is far more fundamental than the intellect. It comes from a different place, a more instinctual place.

It's so fundamental that primates, like chimps, bonobos, and gorillas, practice forgiveness. So do goats, hyenas, dogs, wolves, coyotes, crows, and even rats. Forgiveness and morality are so prevalent at every level of the animal kingdom that scientists credit evolution. Acclaimed primatologist Franz De Wall, in his famous book <u>The Bonobo and the Atheist</u>, makes this claim.

But De Waal, and others like him, aren't looking low enough, or deep enough, to see God.

Forgiveness is wired into our very cells. Expert Everett L. Worthington, Jr. of Virginia Commonwealth University has devoted his entire life to the scientific study of forgiveness. Worthington's research shows that lack of forgiveness for long periods of time leads to elevated blood pressure, heart rate, stress hormone production, and so on. And if those elevations go unchecked, Worthington says, they lead to mental health problems, reliance on alcohol and drugs, elevated cardiovascular risk, digestive, immune, and respiratory problems, sexual and reproductive issues, even physical damage to the structures of the brain.[1]

The need to forgive is in our biology, but it didn't evolve. Saying that forgiveness evolved is like saying that gravity evolved, or magnetism evolved. The laws of physics, and the laws of morality, have been built into the structure of the universe like the bricks in the foundation of a home. Forgiveness is found in the cellular structure of living things *because it's woven into the very fabric of reality by our Heavenly Father.*

But because this world is fallen, God's desire that we forgive – which cries out to us from the very heart of his creation! – is imperfectly heeded by his creatures. Despite the fact that God has embedded the healing power of forgiveness into his universe we too often flee from it. Forgiveness brings peace to survivors of attack, peace to nations, neighborhoods, and broken families. Forgiveness heals hearts, repairs friendships, prevents the escalation of violence, restores harmony between nations, and saves lives.

Let us obey the natural law of forgiveness built into God's creation, and obey the words of our Savior. Let us forgive those who trespass against us not seven times but seventy-seven times.

[1] https://www.templeton.org/wp-content/uploads/2020/06/Forgiveness_final.pdf

25th Sunday of Ordinary Time, Sunday 9/24/23

Readings: Is 55:6-9, Ps 145:2-3, 8-9, 17-18, Phil 1:20c-24, 27a, Mt 20:1-16a

<u>Matthew 20:1-16a World English Bible Catholic Edition</u>

Jesus said, "For the Kingdom of Heaven is like a man who was the master of a household, who went out early in the morning to hire laborers for his vineyard. 2 When he had agreed with the laborers for a denarius† a day, he sent them into his vineyard. 3 He went out about the third hour,‡ and saw others standing idle in the marketplace. 4 He said to them, 'You also go into the vineyard, and whatever is right I will give you.' So they went their way. 5 Again he went out about the sixth and the ninth hour,§ and did likewise. 6 About the eleventh hour† he went out and found others standing idle. He said to them, 'Why do you stand here all day idle?'

7 "They said to him, 'Because no one has hired us.'

"He said to them, 'You also go into the vineyard, and you will receive whatever is right.'

8 "When evening had come, the lord of the vineyard said to his manager, 'Call the laborers and pay them their wages, beginning from the last to the first.' 9 "When those who were

hired at about the eleventh hour came, they each received a denarius. 10 When the first came, they supposed that they would receive more; and they likewise each received a denarius. 11 When they received it, they murmured against the master of the household, 12 saying, 'These last have spent one hour, and you have made them equal to us who have borne the burden of the day and the scorching heat!'

13 "But he answered one of them, 'Friend, I am doing you no wrong. Didn't you agree with me for a denarius? 14 Take that which is yours, and go your way. It is my desire to give to this last just as much as to you. 15 Isn't it lawful for me to do what I want to with what I own? Or is your eye evil, because I am good?' 16 So the last will be first, and the first last."

Friends, there is very little more toxic than a work-and-reward mentality with regard to the spiritual life. Christ, in today's parable, shows us what happens when we fail to get beyond this cumbersome outlook.

We've all had the experience of working alongside someone who has this very simplistic, legalistic mindset. This is the coworker who, when someone gets a promotion at work, says "I've been working here longer. Why didn't I get the position?" This is the teenager who says to his mother, "You let my sister stay out until 11 pm. Why do I have to be home by 9 pm?" Every experienced parent, supervisor, pastor, or leader of any kind recognizes this "it's not fair" outlook as a very sinister poison.

To nip this in the bud, leaders must immediately step in and teach those for whom they are responsible that the thought "it's not fair" should be a call to introspection and faith rather than a call to bitterness. That's what Jesus is doing in today's gospel reading. When we start to think "it's not fair" we should consider that perhaps the quality of our work isn't as good as we think it is. Maybe we need to do better. Or perhaps we just need to be more patient. There could be something amazing coming our way very soon – something that's even better than the thing we're envious about. But, most importantly, we must be mindful that "it's not fair," if left unchecked, becomes the mark of Cain. When God accepted Abel's sacrifice over his, Cain allowed his resentful "it's not fair" attitude to become a motive for murdering his brother. This way of thinking literally points down to hell.

To begin heading upward, we must first see that although we sometimes use the term "the work of the spirit," we should be taking up not a tedious list of chores but a labor of love. This is the pivot point around which the Christian life turns. Jesus said, "'You shall love the Lord your God with all your heart, with all your soul, and with all your mind.' This is the first and greatest commandment. A second likewise is this, 'You shall love your neighbor as yourself.'" (Matthew 22:37-39). And Saint Paul said, "If I give away all my goods to feed the poor, and if I give my body to be burned, but don't have love, it profits me nothing." (1 Cor 13:3).

If we fill up the work of the spirit with love, it becomes a labor of love at which we can work tirelessly. Jealousy and resentment fall away. There is only joy for our brothers and sisters who are successful in both the material life and the spiritual life. We are happy for them at school, at work, in sports, and so on – and when they believe in the Gospel, we are filled with joy at the thought that they might join us in the world to come.

The Christian life is not a call to mere obedience to laws. It is a call to transformation. We are not destined to be laborers in a vineyard, but rather offshoots of the true vine (John 15:1-17). Say goodbye to the "sour grapes" way of life!

† 20:2 A denarius is a silver Roman coin worth 1/25th of a Roman aureus. This was a common wage for a day of farm labor.

‡ 20:3 Time was measured from sunrise to sunset, so the third hour would be about 9:00 a.m.

§ 20:5 noon and 3:00 p.m.

† 20:6 5:00 p.m.

26th Sunday of Ordinary Time, Sunday 10/1/23

Readings: Ez 18:25-28, Ps 25:4-5, 6-7, 8-9, Phil 2:1-11, Mt 21:28-32

<u>Matthew 21:28-32 World English Bible Catholic Edition</u>

Jesus said to the chief priests and to the elders of the people, "But what do you think? A man had two sons, and he came to the first, and said, 'Son, go work today in my vineyard.' 29 He answered, 'I will not,' but afterward he changed his mind, and went. 30 He came to the second, and said the same thing. He answered, 'I'm going, sir,' but he didn't go. 31 Which of the two did the will of his father?"

They said to him, "The first."

Jesus said to them, "Most certainly I tell you that the tax collectors and the prostitutes are entering into God's Kingdom before you. 32 For John came to you in the way of righteousness, and you didn't believe him; but the tax collectors and the prostitutes believed him. When you saw it, you didn't even repent afterward, that you might believe him."

Brothers and sisters, becoming a Christian is not an intellectual decision. Nor is it an emotional feeling, a social or political preference, or an ethical inclination toward a sensible set of moral rules and laws.

Although one or more of those may manifest as a consequence of conversion, they are just phenomena. They are like rain, thunder, and lightning. They are associated with storms, but they are not the storm itself. A storm is a radical change in the upper atmosphere, a fundamental alteration in which huge masses of air are thrust ten or more miles up into the stratosphere. That is what Christianity is: a stratospheric transformation of mind, body, and spirit.

Perhaps the right conditions are beginning to manifest in a person's life and true conversion is close. The Holy Ghost is stirring and the storm is coming. But he or she may see a good person or a young child die, or witnesses a wicked person living a long and materially prosperous life and, as Ezekiel points out, ideas like "It's not fair!" may begin to creep in. But if total transformation in Christ takes place, this person will focus not on material fairness in this world, but on the timeless and precious beauty and joy of participation in Christ consciousness now – and on the ultimate fairness of eternal life in the world to come.

St. Paul describes the transformation that Jesus wants for us as participation in the Spirit; as being of the same mind and in the same love as Jesus, fully united in one heart. Jesus says in today's reading that we must change our minds. He's not looking for us to say the right words or reach the intellectual, moral, social, logical, or emotional conclusions that line up with his teachings. All of that is praiseworthy. We should be able to understand and explain the sensibility and practicality of Christian teachings. But as worthy as all of that may be, it's all just phenomena. It is rain and wind – but not the storm that Jesus is looking for.

When Moses was about to bring down the law, the scripture says that "when it was morning, there were thunders and lightnings, and a thick cloud on the mountain, and the sound of an exceedingly loud trumpet; and all the people who were in the camp trembled." (Exodus 19:16). Although worthy of the awe it inspired, the mighty storm that accompanied the giving of the law is nothing compared to the power and majesty that lifts us up into the heavens and, through unification with Christ, transforms us in body, mind, and spirit.

27th Sunday of Ordinary Time, Sunday 10/8/23

Readings: Is 5:1-7, Ps 80:9, 12, 13-14, 15-16, 19-20, Phil 4:6-9, Mt 21:33-43

<u>Matthew 21:33-43 World English Bible</u>

Jesus said to the chief priests and elders of the people:

"Hear another parable. There was a man who was a master of a household who planted a vineyard, set a hedge about it, dug a wine press in it, built a tower, leased it out to farmers, and went into another country. 34 When the season for the fruit came near, he sent his servants to the farmers to receive his fruit. 35 The farmers took his servants, beat one, killed another, and stoned another. 36 Again, he sent other servants more than the first; and they treated them the same way. 37 But afterward he sent to them his son, saying, 'They will respect my son.' 38 But the farmers, when they saw the son, said among themselves, 'This is the heir. Come, let's kill him and seize his inheritance.' 39 So they took him and threw him out of the vineyard, then killed him. 40 When therefore the lord of the vineyard comes, what will he do to those farmers?"

41 They told him, "He will miserably destroy those miserable men, and will lease out the vineyard to other farmers who will give him the fruit in its season."

234

42 Jesus said to them, "Did you never read in the Scriptures,

'The stone which the builders rejected

was made the head of the corner.

This was from the Lord.

*It is marvelous in our eyes'?**

*43 "Therefore I tell you, God's Kingdom will be taken away
from you and will be given to a nation producing its fruit.
44 He who falls on this stone will be broken to pieces, but on
whomever it will fall, it will scatter him as dust."*

Survival schools teach the importance of a good vantage point. When
lost in the woods, always seek higher ground or climb a tree if you can.
From there you may scan the horizon for paths and roads to follow
home, spot water sources, and see game animals. Modern hunters use
tree stands in the same way that ancient hunters sat or stood in trees
with spears and bows. Soldiers also seek the high ground to see enemies
approaching from miles away. A city on a hill is more easily defended.
The high ground is always an advantage. Having an *advantage* and
having a good *vantage* point are so tightly related that they have the
same root word.

In the Garden of Eden God placed the tree of knowledge and the
tree of life. Every tree is in some way a tree of knowledge because from
its branches we gain information about our surroundings. Every tree is
a tree of life because climbing its branches yields nourishment (spotting
prey and picking fruit) and provides safety (tactical vantage).

Because we live in a world in which our food comes from a market
and our defense is provided by police and armies, these things are no

longer obvious to us. But for ancient peoples, all of this would have been glaring. Fruit on the ground is unhealthy to eat and could be a trap laid by enemies lurking above. A clever enemy attacks during the harvest when defenses are down and crops are gathered, ripe for the taking. Wise people climb up into the branches of the tree or to the top of the tower, to spot the best fruit, the choicest game, and the approaching enemy. All of this would have stood out to the people of the past as starkly as a plume of smoke spotted from a high hill. Adam, Eve, and the bad tenants of the landowner's vineyard are of the same type. These characters are shortsighted, rapacious, taking what they want today at the expense of the longer view. All are given a garden which they fail to tend as they have been instructed by the landowner. Lost in the woods, they'd be dead in no time.

Isaiah and Jesus didn't put the tower into their stories as a mere embellishment or a nice touch of color. A man-made garden like a vineyard calls for a man-made tree. So, in the center of the garden, the landowner builds a tower. The vineyard is a garden which, like Eden, is made by a loving father for the benefit of those capable of appreciating its perfection. The servants hired to tend the vineyard never bother to ascend the tower and see the majesty of the work the landowner has built for them to tend. Adam and Eve never climbed the tree of knowledge. They stood on the ground and seized the fruit. Had they first climbed up to survey Eden, they would have gained the vision and patience to wait for God's permission to eat the fruit and there would've been no fall.

Friends, let us endeavor to be as wise as the ancient Semitic people whose oral stories are recorded in the book of Genesis. Let us endeavor to spot the details of the story that the people of Jesus' time would've noticed right away. Greed, covetousness, laziness, violence, these are the low-hanging fruits of sin and death. Attempting to see the world from God's higher vantage point is the way to eternal life.

* 21:42 Psalm 118:22-23

28th Sunday of Ordinary Time, Sunday 10/15/23

Readings: Is 25:6-10a, Ps 23:1-3a, 3b-4, 5, 6, Phil 4:12-14, 19-20, Mt 22:1-14

<u>Matthew 22: 1-14 World English Bible Catholic Edition</u>

Jesus answered and spoke to them again in parables, saying, 2 "The Kingdom of Heaven is like a certain king, who made a wedding feast for his son, 3 and sent out his servants to call those who were invited to the wedding feast, but they would not come. 4 Again he sent out other servants, saying, 'Tell those who are invited, "Behold, I have prepared my dinner. My cattle and my fatlings are killed, and all things are ready. Come to the wedding feast!" ' 5 But they made light of it, and went their ways, one to his own farm, another to his merchandise; 6 and the rest grabbed his servants, treated them shamefully, and killed them. 7 When the king heard that, he was angry, and sent his armies, destroyed those murderers, and burned their city.

8 "Then he said to his servants, 'The wedding is ready, but those who were invited weren't worthy. 9 Go therefore to the intersections of the highways, and as many as you may find, invite to the wedding feast.' 10 Those servants went out into the highways and gathered together as many as they found, both bad and good. The wedding was filled with guests.

11 "But when the king came in to see the guests, he saw there a man who didn't have on wedding clothing, 12 and he said to him, 'Friend, how did you come in here not wearing wedding clothing?' He was speechless. 13 Then the king said to the servants, 'Bind him hand and foot, take him away, and throw him into the outer darkness. That is where the weeping and grinding of teeth will be.' 14 For many are called, but few chosen."

"For many are called, but few are chosen." These words reverberate to us down the two millennia since our Savior spoke them. What is the proper interpretation? Should we use them to think of ourselves as an elite club? Some experts suggest that by "chosen" we should interpret "elected." Are we "chosen" the way that certain politicians are "elected" to office? Are we "chosen" in the same way that the best athletes are drafted onto sports teams?

To grapple with this question, we should consider first and foremost that there are only so many open seats in a government, and only so many open positions on a sports team. To elect an official to a position is to exclude everyone else. The same is true, let's say, in football. There are only so many players in the league. Everyone else is on the sidelines. This is the way it is with human beings and our ways. In our games, there is always a winner and a loser.

But not so with the kingdom of God. His realm is infinite in scope. In John 14:2 we hear, "In my father's house are many mansions." God's separation of the unchosen from the chosen is not an act of exclusion or elitism because in his kingdom there is enough room for everyone. Choosing one does not exclude another. God sent his only begotten son Jesus Christ to bring everyone to the banquet. His love for humanity is so great that he wants everyone to stay for the festivities. He loves us so much, and so badly wants no one to be left out, that he gave each and every one of us the capacity to be chosen. All we have to do is genuinely show up and participate.

In Jesus' parable, he equates our choice to dressing appropriately for a banquet. I'm sure you've been to events where there are people in attendance who don't even try. The invitation says "semi-formal attire" but they show up in blue jeans and T-shirts. Few notice or comment, not even the hosts, on a suit or a dress that's a little out of style or a touch threadbare. All they have to do is put in a little bit of effort. But for these people, that's just too much to ask. I think that's what Jesus is trying to get across in this parable. We don't have to be perfect to be chosen by God – all we have to do is sincerely try to follow him and live his ways, to genuinely attempt to give ourselves over to his saving grace. We can't be truly holy as God is holy – fair enough. But we can at least be baptized, step into the robe, and make a sincere attempt to clothe ourselves in holiness.

In Luke 17:21 we read, "Neither shall they say, Lo here! or, lo there! for, behold, the kingdom of God is within you." Inside of each of us, God has graced us with the capacity to listen to his Word, accept his teaching, and stay through the banquet to the end. The choice is ours.

29th Sunday of Ordinary Time, Sunday 10/22/23

Readings: Is 45:1, 4-6, Ps 96:1, 3, 4-5, 7-8, 9-10, 1 Thes 1:1-5b, Mt 22:15-21

Matthew 22:15-21 World English Bible Catholic Edition

Then the Pharisees went and took counsel how they might entrap him in his talk. 16 They sent their disciples to him, along with the Herodians, saying, "Teacher, we know that you are honest, and teach the way of God in truth, no matter whom you teach; for you aren't partial to anyone. 17 Tell us therefore, what do you think? Is it lawful to pay taxes to Caesar, or not?"

18 But Jesus perceived their wickedness, and said, "Why do you test me, you hypocrites? 19 Show me the tax money."

They brought to him a denarius.

20 He asked them, "Whose is this image and inscription?"

21 They said to him, "Caesar's."

Then he said to them, "Give therefore to Caesar the things that are Caesar's, and to God the things that are God's."

22 When they heard it, they marveled, and left him and went away.

God reminds King Cyrus, Cyrus the Great, in our first reading, "I have given you a title, though you have not known me...I will strengthen you, though you have not known me...that there is no one besides me. I am the LORD, and there is no one else." This is Cyrus, who the Jews called *messiah* after he ended their Babylonian captivity and welcomed them back to their homeland of Judah. And he is being reminded that he is a "a king" not "the King." History is God's production, and even Cyrus the Great is just an actor in the play. He may be at the top of the ladder of his realm, but he is just one of many kings allowed to have authority in God's grand hierarchy.

The Bible has a lot to say about what happens when people, groups, nations, and kings improperly conceive hierarchies and their places within them. We need look no further than Pharaoh in the Book of Exodus, whose tyrannical hubris ends in the death of every firstborn son of Egypt, including his own, and destruction of his army. Kings and leaders should remember that they are not at the top of the pyramid – God is – and rulership constitutes a responsibility in God's order.

This is why, in our epistle reading, St. Paul writes to the Thessalonians on behalf of himself, Silvanus, and Timothy, as an aligned group of peers, not as a sovereign, a commander, or a dictator. And rather than ordering allegiance, he thanks the Thessalonian church for their "work of labor and love" and offers his prayers for them. This is the way God wants leaders to function – not as privileged dictators, but as servants of God seeking what is best for all.

In Matthew 22:15-21, the Pharisees ask Jesus a trick question concerning the hierarchical relationship between Jewish citizens and the emperor of Rome. If Jesus says they shouldn't pay their taxes to Caesar, he'll be liable to the Roman charge of treason. If he says they should pay them, he'll be supporting the empire's oppression. Jesus' sarcastic answer cuts to the heart of the matter. "Whose picture is on the money? Caesar? Okay, so give him what's his." Then he adds that we should give to God what is God's. What are we supposed to render to

God? Our commandment is, "You shall love the Lord your God with all your heart, with all your soul, and with all your mind." (Mat 22:37, Deut 6:5). Caesar is just a ruler who has his face on Roman money. God is worthy of our total faith, hope, and love.

If you think the founding fathers of the United States of America didn't thoroughly grasp these biblical lessons, you're mistaken. On the front of our one-dollar bill there is no Caesar. Instead there is our first President, George Washington, a public servant. On the back of the bill there are no pictures of Caesar and his war chariots. Instead, there is an Egyptian pyramid, the top of which has been cut off. Pharaoh has been cast down and replaced with the all-seeing eye of our Heavenly Father. Roman coins declared the godhood of Tiberius Caesar. Our bill says, "In God We Trust."

In this world there can be no utopia. But time and again we find that things go best when we remember that God is the source and summit of all. As we are reminded in the doxology, "Through Him, with Him and in Him, in the unity of the Holy Spirit, all glory and honor is yours, almighty Father, for ever and ever. Amen."

30th Sunday of Ordinary Time, Sunday 10/29/23

Readings: Ex 22:20-26, Ps 18:2-3, 3-4, 47, 51, 1 Thes 1:5c-10, Mt 22:34-40

Matthew 22:34-40 World English Bible Catholic Edition

But the Pharisees, when they heard that he had silenced the Sadducees, gathered themselves together. 35 One of them, a lawyer, asked him a question, testing him. 36 "Teacher, which is the greatest commandment in the law?"

37 Jesus said to him, " 'You shall love the Lord your God with all your heart, with all your soul, and with all your mind.' 38 This is the first and great commandment. 39 A second likewise is this, 'You shall love your neighbor as yourself.'* 40 The whole law and the prophets depend on these two commandments."*

"There are two paths, one of life and one of death, and the difference is great between the two paths. Now the path of life is this—first, thou shalt love the God who made thee, thy neighbour as thyself, and all things that thou wouldest not have done unto thee, do not thou unto another. And the doctrine of these maxims is as follows. Bless them that curse you, and pray for your enemies. Fast on behalf of those that persecute you; for what thank is there if ye love them that love you? Do not even the Gentiles do the same? But love them that hate you, and ye will not have an enemy. Abstain from fleshly and worldly lusts. If any one give thee a blow on thy right cheek, turn unto him the other also, and thou shalt be perfect; if any one compel thee to go a mile, go with him two; if a man take away thy cloak, give him thy coat also; if a man take from thee what is thine, ask not for it again, for neither art thou able to do so. Give to every one that asketh of thee, and ask not again, for the Father wishes that from his own gifts there should be given to all.

My child, fly from everything that is evil, and from everything that is like to it. Thou shalt not exalt thyself, neither shalt thou put boldness into thy soul. Thy soul shall not be joined unto the lofty, but thou shalt walk with the just and humble. Accept the things that happen to thee as good, knowing that without God nothing happens.

Seek out day by day the favor of the saints, that thou mayest rest in their words; thou shalt not desire schism, but shalt set at peace them that contend; thou shalt not abandon the commandments of the Lord, but shalt guard that which thou hast received, neither adding thereto nor taking therefrom; thou shalt confess thy transgressions in the church, and shalt not come unto prayer with an evil conscience. This is the path of life.

But the path of death is this. First of all, it is evil and full of cursing; there are found murders, adulteries, lusts, fornication, thefts, idolatries, soothsaying, sorceries, robberies, false witnessings, hypocrisies, double-mindedness, craft, pride, malice, self-will, covetousness, filthy talking, jealousy, audacity, arrogance; there are they who persecute the good—lovers of a lie, not knowing the reward of righteousness, not cleaving to the good nor to righteous judgment, watching not for the good but for the bad, from whom meekness and patience are afar off, loving things that are vain, following after recompense, having no compassion on the needy, nor laboring for him that is in trouble, not knowing him that made them, murderers of children, corrupters of the image of God, who turn away from him that is in need, who oppress him that is in trouble, unjust judges of the poor, erring in all things. From all these, children, may ye be delivered."[1]

Brothers and sisters, the words I have just shared with you are almost two thousand years old, and they are excerpted from a short book known as the *The Didache*, which means "the teaching," and was written in the first century after the Resurrection. It is considered the first book of Christian teaching. I hope you can see how it illustrates that, since the earliest days of the church, loving God and our neighbor has been the core of Christian teaching.

* 22:37 Deuteronomy 6:5

[1] Charles Hoole, *The Didache* (London: Nutt, 1894) pp 75-79. Available online at https://archive.org/details/didacheorteachin00hool/page/n1/mode/2up

All Souls Day, Sunday 11/5/23

Readings: Isaiah 25:6-10a, Psalm 103:8,10,13-14,15-16,17-18, Romans 8:31b-39, John 6:51-58

<u>John 6:51-58 World English Bible Catholic Edition</u>

Jesus said, "I am the living bread which came down out of heaven. If anyone eats of this bread, he will live forever. Yes, the bread which I will give for the life of the world is my flesh."

52 The Jews therefore contended with one another, saying, "How can this man give us his flesh to eat?"

53 Jesus therefore said to them, "Most certainly I tell you, unless you eat the flesh of the Son of Man and drink his blood, you don't have life in yourselves. 54 He who eats my flesh and drinks my blood has eternal life, and I will raise him up at the last day. 55 For my flesh is food indeed, and my blood is drink indeed. 56 He who eats my flesh and drinks my blood lives in me, and I in him. 57 As the living Father sent me, and I live because of the Father, so he who feeds on me will also live because of me. 58 This is the bread which came down out of heaven—not as our fathers ate the manna and died. He who eats this bread will live forever."

Across a hundred millennia, humanity has developed a myriad of theories about death – reincarnation, metempsychosis, Norse Valhalla, Greek Hades, Jewish *sheol*, and so forth. In like manner, the fathers of the Christian church, starting with the apostle Paul and flowing downstream, espoused a truly unique viewpoint.

They began with the idea that nothing can move directly from pre-existence into being. Their logic was simple. You can't say, "On March the 12th Fred went from being nothing to being something" because, prior to March the 12th, there was no Fred. "Being nothing" is a contradiction. Fred can't move from nothingness to somethingness because there was no Fred to move. Something cannot materialize out of nothing.

Drawing on Aristotle and Plato's concept of forms, the Christian church fathers – St. Gregory of Nyssa, St. Thomas Aquinas, St. Augustine, and many others – elegantly solved the problem of creation in the following way. Fred is *caused*. He grew out of the material contributions of his father and mother. Everything has a cause. Otherwise people, objects, animals, and so on would just pop into and out of existence. But, they posited, if we trace Fred back a bit farther, he began with a gleam in his parents' eye. This is a third state of being sometimes referred to as the *prima materia*, Latin for "first matter." This is the state of non-being or potential. We all acknowledge this state when we say things like, "Fred is not living up to his potential" or when we look at a dingy dresser and see what it could be with a coat of paint.

First matter is like an object over which a sheet is draped. If you throw a sheet over a chair, the sheet resembles a chair. If you lay it over a bust of Edgar Allen Poe, it looks like Poe. Anyone who makes or creates anything first works in the realm of potential, conceiving a work of art, a song, a building, an invention, etc. If there was no potential, then nothing could become. The engine of reality would cease to run, and Being itself would cease to be. Only God, as the first cause, can bring something out of nothing. He brought into being potential itself, the *prima materia*, and this state of potential is the foundation upon which existence rests.

In Genesis 3:21, after Adam and Eve have eaten the forbidden fruit, we read, "The LORD God made garments of animal skins for Adam and for his wife, and clothed them." Because they sinned, our first parents were given corruptible skins, bodies that deteriorate. This is a metaphor for the fact that everything that exists in the universe now has a "corruptible skin." All things die, all metals oxidize and rust, all foods rot, and all suns burn out. All things decay.[1]

The miracle of Christian theology is at once starkly logical and filled with the beauty, hope, and love of the Holy Ghost. St. Paul sums all this up in Romans 4:17, saying that God, "gives life to the dead and calls into being what does not exist."

My friends, Fred's birth is the draping of his potential with a sheet – the receiving of his imperfect garment of skin. Conversely, his death is his undraping. When Fred dies, he doesn't cease to exist – he merely goes back to the realm of potential, back to *prima materia*. And there he remains, awaiting the blessed hope of the resurrection when, by the grace of God, he may realize his full potential and receive a new and incorruptible garment of glory.

[1] St. Gregory of Nyssa said, "Likewise, when we have put off that dead and ugly garment that was made for us from irrational skins…we throw off every part of our irrational skin along with the removal of the garment." And St. Augustine said, "Adam and Eve, who were stripped of their first garment of innocence, deserved by their mortality garments of skin. For the true honor of man is to be the image and the likeness of God." https://catenabible.com/gn/3

32nd Sunday in Ordinary Time, Sunday 11/12/23

Readings: Wis 6:12-16, Ps 63:2, 3-4, 5-6, 7-8, 1 Thes 4:13-18, Mt 25:1-13

<u>Matthew 25:1-13 World English Bible</u>

Jesus said, "Then the Kingdom of Heaven will be like ten virgins who took their lamps and went out to meet the bridegroom. 2 Five of them were foolish, and five were wise. 3 Those who were foolish, when they took their lamps, took no oil with them, 4 but the wise took oil in their vessels with their lamps. 5 Now while the bridegroom delayed, they all slumbered and slept. 6 But at midnight there was a cry, 'Behold! The bridegroom is coming! Come out to meet him!' 7 Then all those virgins arose, and trimmed their lamps.† 8 The foolish said to the wise, 'Give us some of your oil, for our lamps are going out.' 9 But the wise answered, saying, 'What if there isn't enough for us and you? You go rather to those who sell, and buy for yourselves.' 10 While they went away to buy, the bridegroom came, and those who were ready went in with him to the wedding feast, and the door was shut. 11 Afterward the other virgins also came, saying, 'Lord, Lord, open to us.' 12 But he answered, 'Most certainly I tell you, I don't know you.' 13 Watch therefore, for you don't know the day nor the hour in which the Son of Man is coming.

What is a virgin? A young woman who has not lain with a man, symbolizing a man or woman who is not promiscuous. This is someone who is in control of his or her behavior. Ten is the number of the Ten Commandments, what the Hebrews called "The Ten Words" or "The Ten Sayings" and ten is the number associated with *malkut*, the Jewish mystical concept of physical creation.

Thus we see that the ten virgins are all following the rules. They are pure in their worldly behavior. But self-control, although praiseworthy, faces inward. Discipline is a type of light, but it is a containment rather than an outpouring of light. It's also necessary for the spirit that inspired the discipline to have an outburst. The virgins, therefore, carry lamps so that their light can shine forth.

This part of the parable is an echo of Matthew 5:14-16. *"You are the light of the world. A city located on a hill can't be hidden. Neither do you light a lamp and put it under a bushel basket, but on a stand; and it shines to all who are in the house. Even so, let your light shine before men, that they may see your good works and glorify your Father who is in heaven."* It's not enough for us to be in control of our behavior. We must go into the world and shine our light into dark places, into prisons, hospitals, and churches, into the lives of disordered people, and into the structures of benighted institutions, filling them with God's light: Goodness, Beauty, and Truth, Faith, Hope, and Love.

In Jesus' parable, all of the virgins fall asleep. We are all imperfect. We are bound to need rest, and our focus is destined to wax and wane. But if we are wise, we will be ready with extra reserves of fuel. We won't, like the foolish virgins, expect others to give us some of their oil. But what is this mysterious oil, and what is this lamp we are expected to carry?

The oil is the understanding and acceptance of Jesus Christ as our savior who lives in us and in whom we live. We can't just follow the laws and be virgins. St. Paul says in Galatians 2:19-20, "For I through the law died to the law, that I might live to God. I have been crucified with Christ, and it is no longer I who live, but Christ lives in me. That life which I now live in the flesh, I live by faith in the Son of God, who loved me and gave himself up for me." We can't do this ourselves. We must be fueled by union with him.

And what is the lamp? In Revelation 21:23 we read that the New Jerusalem, "has no need for the sun or moon to shine, for the very glory of God illuminated it and its lamp is the Lamb." As we await our Savior's return, let us hold high the light of the Christ and let it shine into every dark place.

† 25:7 The end of the wick of an oil lamp needs to be cut off periodically to avoid having it become clogged with carbon deposits. The wick height is also adjusted so that the flame burns evenly and gives good light without producing a lot of smoke.

Ecce Agnus Dei qui tollit peccata mundi

–

"Behold the Lamb of God who takest away the sins of the world."

33rd Sunday in Ordinary Time, Sunday 11/19/23

Readings: Prv 31:10-13, 19-20, 30-31, Ps 128:1-2, 3, 4-5, 1 Thes 5:1-6, Mt 25:14-30

<u>Matthew 25:14-30 World English Bible Catholic Edition</u>

14 *"For it is like a man going into another country, who called his own servants and entrusted his goods to them. 15 To one he gave five talents,‡ to another two, to another one, to each according to his own ability. Then he went on his journey. 16 Immediately he who received the five talents went and traded with them, and made another five talents. 17 In the same way, he also who got the two gained another two. 18 But he who received the one talent went away and dug in the earth and hid his lord's money.*

19 *"Now after a long time the lord of those servants came, and settled accounts with them. 20 He who received the five talents came and brought another five talents, saying, 'Lord, you delivered to me five talents. Behold, I have gained another five talents in addition to them.'*

21 *"His lord said to him, 'Well done, good and faithful servant. You have been faithful over a few things, I will set you over many things. Enter into the joy of your lord.'*

22 "He also who got the two talents came and said, 'Lord, you delivered to me two talents. Behold, I have gained another two talents in addition to them.'

23 "His lord said to him, 'Well done, good and faithful servant. You have been faithful over a few things. I will set you over many things. Enter into the joy of your lord.'

24 "He also who had received the one talent came and said, 'Lord, I knew you that you are a hard man, reaping where you didn't sow, and gathering where you didn't scatter. 25 I was afraid, and went away and hid your talent in the earth. Behold, you have what is yours.'

26 "But his lord answered him, 'You wicked and slothful servant. You knew that I reap where I didn't sow, and gather where I didn't scatter. 27 You ought therefore to have deposited my money with the bankers, and at my coming I should have received back my own with interest. 28 Take away therefore the talent from him and give it to him who has the ten talents. 29 For to everyone who has will be given, and he will have abundance, but from him who doesn't have, even that which he has will be taken away. 30 Throw out the unprofitable servant into the outer darkness, where there will be weeping and gnashing of teeth.'

Some years ago I was a mid-level accounting manager looking to hire a file person. I got a stack of resumes from the Virginia Employment Commission's special placements section for handicapped people. I asked the VEC to bring them in for interviews.

The first few didn't show much promise. But then in walked Alice.[1] She wasn't very articulate, but she was a smiling bundle of enthusiasm. It was like sitting across the table from a slice of golden sunshine. So I decided to give her a little test. I led her to the file room down the hall, handed her about a hundred invoices, and asked her to put them in numerical order. Then I went back to the conference room. I barely had enough time to sit down and exchange a sentence or two with the VEC representatives before Alice was back. I assumed she was confused or had a question. But no – she was finished.

I flipped through the pile. There were no errors I could see. Sensing my shock at her speed and accuracy, the VEC folks explained that Alice grasped number sequences intuitively, like colors or smells. We all chatted a bit. Alice explained that her children were now in school and she was looking to enter the workforce for the first time. She wanted to bring in some money so that her husband Charlie wouldn't have to work so hard. She hoped that, with her help, the could perhaps get ahead. She said that she had been looking for a job for a very long time, but nobody had given her the time of day.

I gave her the position on the spot. I would've been a fool not to. She was tailormade for putting papers in numerical order, and to her, this monotonous job was a golden opportunity. She worked for me for many years. And in time she learned to do more. She filled in for our receptionist, greeted customers, answered calls, and so on.

Like Alice, we are all given certain talents. Make no mistake – the word *talent*, as in a natural, in-born gift, is literally the same word as a *talent*, a standard weight of silver in the ancient world. They are not, by any means, different words that happen to sound the same. *They are the same word.* A talent – a skill – is money in the bank. Unless of course we bury it in the ground like the third servant, who takes the one talent of silver his master gives him and puts it where it cannot multiply.

The master shuts this lazy man out, leaving him in the cold and dark. Don't you see? That could've been Alice. Imagine how hard it must've been for an adult woman with learning disabilities and no experience to go out and try to find a job. God gave Alice one talent. Did she bury it? No, no! She was brave. She took a courageous risk, and it paid off. Not just for her and her family, but for me, my business, and everyone who got to see her smile.

We are all given talents by our creator, and we are supposed to put them to good use, not just for ourselves, but for the good of everyone – for our coworkers, our communities, our churches, and ultimately, for the greater glory of God.

[1] Her name is not Alice. Name changed to maintain anonymity.

The Solemnity of Our Lord Jesus Christ, King of the Universe, Sunday 11/26/23

Readings: Ez 34:11-12, 15-17, Ps 23:1-2, 2-3, 5-6, 1 Cor 15:20-26, 28, Mt 25:31-46

Matthew 25:31-46 World English Bible Catholic Edition

Jesus said to his disciples, "But when the Son of Man comes in his glory, and all the holy angels with him, then he will sit on the throne of his glory. 32 Before him all the nations will be gathered, and he will separate them one from another, as a shepherd separates the sheep from the goats. 33 He will set the sheep on his right hand, but the goats on the left. 34 Then the King will tell those on his right hand, 'Come, blessed of my Father, inherit the Kingdom prepared for you from the foundation of the world; 35 for I was hungry and you gave me food to eat. I was thirsty and you gave me drink. I was a stranger and you took me in. 36 I was naked and you clothed me. I was sick and you visited me. I was in prison and you came to me.'

37 "Then the righteous will answer him, saying, 'Lord, when did we see you hungry and feed you, or thirsty and give you a drink? 38 When did we see you as a stranger and take you in, or naked and clothe you? 39 When did we see you sick or in prison and come to you?'

40 "The King will answer them, 'Most certainly I tell you, because you did it to one of the least of these my brothers,§ you did it to me.' 41 Then he will say also to those on the left hand, 'Depart from me, you cursed, into the eternal fire which is prepared for the devil and his angels; 42 for I was hungry, and you didn't give me food to eat; I was thirsty, and you gave me no drink; 43 I was a stranger, and you didn't take me in; naked, and you didn't clothe me; sick, and in prison, and you didn't visit me.'

44 "Then they will also answer, saying, 'Lord, when did we see you hungry, or thirsty, or a stranger, or naked, or sick, or in prison, and didn't help you?'

45 "Then he will answer them, saying, 'Most certainly I tell you, because you didn't do it to one of the least of these, you didn't do it to me.' 46 These will go away into eternal punishment, but the righteous into eternal life."

Brothers and sisters, God is a unifier. He wants to "seek that which was lost" to "bring back that which was driven away," to "bind up that which was broken." (Ez 34:16). He wants to join and mend. The devil, on the other hand, is a divider. He is diabolic. Diabolic comes from Latin. It literally means *di-*, which is "two" and *abolere*, "to abolish, destroy, annihilate." The devil wants to divide and conquer God's flock. And, with our willing cooperation, he has done a masterful job.

Satan's first success was the Great Schism of 1054, in which there arose between the Western and Eastern churches a two-pronged argument over the proper understanding and expression of the Nicene Creed and whether or not the bread used during Mass should be leavened or unleavened. This is how the Devil works. Knowing how badly we want to be right, he uses the idolatrous bait-and-switch. He offered each side the opportunity to worship the subject of the dispute rather than God himself, and both sides took the bait.

The devil's second great diabolic success was the Protestant reformation. In response to serious corruption and misdeeds, reformers from within leveled sincere, valid, and much-needed criticisms against the Western church. But soon both sides took the devil's bait and began to worship their positions rather than God. And this split, by far the evil one's greatest victory so far, was the first domino in a series of cascading, ever-toppling, still-unfolding schisms.

The evil one's third triumph will be the destruction of the world's largest Christian denomination, the Roman Catholic Church. Even now, many arguments are brewing, the most contentious and petty being over whether or not the Mass should be said in Latin. It's approaching fever pitch. The more the Church attempts to force all believers to perform Mass in native languages, the more traditionalists cleave to Latin. Once again, the devil is performing his diabolic bait and switch, tempting each side to worship the words they speak rather than the Word who created the universe.

Notice brothers, and sisters how, in today's Gospel reading, Jesus says that at the Last Judgment, both sides will say the same thing: "Lord, when did we see you hungry, or thirsty, or a stranger, or naked, or sick, or in prison"? In this great teaching, Jesus tells us that, in the end, both the righteous and the unrighteous are ignorant of the fact that how we love our neighbor is the measure of how we love God.

We would be wise to remember that the God's first commandment is "Thou shalt have no other gods before me" or as Jesus restated it in the Gospel, "You shall love the Lord your God with all your heart, with all your soul, with all your mind, and with all your strength. This is the first commandment." (Mark 12:30). Only our King, who will come again, can judge between the quick and the dead – between those who are alive in love for him and those who are dead in their love for their own devices.

§ 25:40 The word for "brothers" here may be also correctly translated "brothers and sisters" or "siblings."

[1] Line numbers vary between translations of this passage due to the inclusion/omission of certain lines depending on the original manuscript.

Don't miss out!

Visit the website below and you can sign up to receive emails whenever Robert Mitchell publishes a new book. There's no charge and no obligation.

https://books2read.com/r/B-A-PFAU-ZUHZC

BOOKS 2 READ

Connecting independent readers to independent writers.

About the Author

Robert Mitchell is a priest in the Old Catholic tradition from Richmond, VA. He is the founder of Heritage Arts Inc., a 501(c)(3) federally-recognized non-profit educational charity providing free instruction in martial arts, fitness, outdoor skills, and spiritual development (www.heritageartsinc.com). A martial artist for over thirty-five years, in 2011 he was awarded the rank of Master by the Combat Martial Arts Practitioners Association, and in 2019 became an authorized instructor of Mark Hatmaker's Frontier Rough & Tumble Martial arts program.

His writing credits include two books of homilies -- "Lift up Your Heads: A Year of Old Catholic Homilies" and "Seek His Face: Another Year of Old Catholic Homilies" -- the martial arts book "Martial Grit: Real Fighting Fitness on a Budget," the fitness bestseller "The Calisthenics Codex" (which has been in Smashword's Top 10 fitness books since its publication in 2015) and "The Wildwood Workbook: Nature Appreciation and Survival." His fiction work includes novels, poems, 'zines, comic books, and short pieces which have appeared in the Journal of Asian Martial Arts, Hulltown 360 Literary Journal, and others.He graduated from the University of Virginia in 1983 with a B.A. in English. He and his wife are the proud parents of four children and five grandchildren.

Read more at https://www.heritageartsinc.com/.

www.ingramcontent.com/pod-product-compliance
Lightning Source LLC
Chambersburg PA
CBHW061429150726
47987CB00001B/148